FOOLPROOF

BBQ

FOOLPROOF

BBQ

60 SIMPLE RECIPES TO MAKE
THE MOST OF YOUR BARBECUE

GENEVIEVE TAYLOR

PHOTOGRAPHY BY
JASON INGRAM

Hardie Grant

QUADRILLE

Publishing Director
Sarah Lavelle

Editor
Stacey Cleworth

Copy-editor
Susan Low

**Art Direction
and Design**
Emily Lapworth

Photographer
Jason Ingram

Food Stylist
Genevieve Taylor

Prop Stylist
Jaine Bevan

Head of Production
Stephen Lang

**Senior Production
Controller**
Katie Jarvis

First published in 2021 by Quadrille,
an imprint of Hardie Grant Publishing

Quadrille
52–54 Southwark Street
London SE1 1UN
quadrille.com

Cataloguing in Publication Data: a catalogue
record for this book is available from the
British Library.

978 1 78713 671 7

Printed in China

CONTENTS

INTRODUCTION

Welcome to *Foolproof BBQ*, a rather useful collection of colourful, varied, easy recipes that will inspire you to get grilling all year round. You cannot beat the taste of food cooked outside. The high heat causes deep caramelization and creates irresistibly crispy, charred edges. Barbecuing also injects a little theatre into your life. Cooking over fire is my passion, and it allows me many culinary adventures.

This book is 'foolproof' because none of the recipes is too taxing to shop for, or to cook. I have a range of barbecues of different shapes and sizes, from fancy to budget, hi-tech to basic. All the recipes were cooked on a standard kettle barbecue with a lid.

Many of the recipes contain just a handful of easily found ingredients. For some, the ingredients list is a little longer, but all should be available from a good-sized supermarket. A quick shop online will help for one or two more unusual things – *pul biber* pepper flakes, or proper Mexican corn tortillas, for example. If you are short of time, just cut a few corners occasionally. This is not 'cheating' – it is sensible, realistic cooking. Use store-bought spice rubs and pastes, buy in coleslaw and dips and sauces.

One way to make barbecuing foolproof is to get ahead. Prep everything you need in the kitchen in one go, then have it lined up and ready by the barbecue before you begin cooking.

The other way to make things easier is to practise. If you drag a dusty grill out of your garage twice a summer, it will probably always feel more challenging than foolproof.

Barbecue a little more regularly and you will gain confidence each time you fire up – and with confidence will come a desire to experiment and learn more. I have been cooking this way for years and I'm still learning. I still get things wrong occasionally but, importantly, I have equipped myself with the basic skills to adapt and work with the heat I have.

The fundamental skill needed for barbecuing success is understanding how to work with the heat. There is no knob to turn up or down to moderate temperature as there is in your kitchen – but you can create different heat zones. The easiest way is to learn the difference between direct and indirect cooking over the heat source. I explain this in more detail on page 9.

I try not to categorize food as 'barbecue food'. Think of the fire in your barbecue as simply your heat source, just as you would your hob (stovetop) or electric oven. Once you grab hold of that mindset, you will realize that pretty much everything can be barbecued.

Fire is the original cooking tool. There is not a corner of the world that doesn't have a history of cooking over live fire. For that reason many of these recipes are global in their reach, full of spices and herbs that bring food alive.

I hope this book provides you with inspiration and sets you on a glorious journey to grilling heaven!

@GenevieveEats

Barbecue hardware

You can grill or barbecue on anything you can light a fire in – even a metal bucket with an old oven grill on top would do. You don't need a lot of fancy equipment. At a minimum, I suggest seeking out a grill/barbecue that has a lid. Put the lid down, and you get even, efficient, oven-like heat. You wouldn't light your oven inside and expect to cook with the door open – and grilling is the same. A lid allows you to use your fuel more wisely.

Fuel matters

This book was written with cooking over charcoal firmly in mind – but that is not to say you can't get brilliant results on a gas barbecue, or even in your kitchen if you prefer. Adapting these recipes for a gas barbecue is easy. Rather than using direct or indirect heat (see Essential Techniques, page 9), you just turn the temperature dial up or down. For cooking indoors, a cast-iron griddle pan or a fireproof frying pan (skillet) on the hob (stovetop) works best. For slow-cooked dishes, use your oven.

Charcoal

Charcoal is your single most important ingredient. The success of your cooking and the flavour of your food will rely on it. Sustainably produced charcoal is unrivalled for cooking, and contains no nasty chemicals or additives, and has environmental and economic benefits too. Most mass-produced charcoal is made from tropical hardwoods and often contains chemicals that need burning off before cooking. The myth of cooking out your charcoal until it is white and ashed over is something you only need to do for cheap charcoal, to burn off any additives. With sustainable lumpwood charcoal, you can light it and be cooking on it in no time. Look online for suppliers of sustainable fuel. It costs more but it's worth every penny.

Adding smoke

The very best charcoal is 95% carbon and, once lit, is smokeless. If you want to add smoke, you need to add wood. I generally use chunks of wood rather than wood chips. Wood chips made for smoking burn hot and fast, and the effect of the smoke dissipates too quickly for maximum effect. You can dampen the chips to slow the process down, but damp chips release a dirty, soggy smoulder. One or two chunks of pure wood placed on top of the hot coals will ignite efficiently and create wafts of beautiful smoke to flavour your food. If you're using a gas grill, wrap a bundle of wood chips in foil, pierce a few holes through the parcel and put onto the flames.

Lighting the fire

A chimney starter is the quickest, most efficient way to light your barbecue. I rarely light a barbecue without one. Chimney starters are easy to find online or in DIY shops or hardware stores. You fill them up with charcoal and place a single natural fire lighter under the base. The air quickly draws up from the bottom through to the top, igniting your fuel. Once the fuel is lit halfway up the chimney, tip the lit fuel into the base of your grill and begin cooking. With good charcoal and a chimney starter, you can be cooking in 10 minutes. Invest in natural fire lighters made from pure wood shavings and wax. These contain none of the chemicals used in the old-style (and very smelly) white cubes. They are easy to find online and in some supermarkets.

Key

Vegetarian (V), vegan (VE) and pescatarian (P) recipes have been marked as such. Additional recipes could be adapted so that they are suitable for vegetarians by simply swapping specific ingredients for an alternative.

EQUIPMENT

Some equipment is essential, some merely useful. In order of priority:

Digital probe thermometer

Essential. Invest in one and you can be confident that your meat is cooked safely and to your liking. When barbecuing, the internal tempearure is the best gauge, rather than a set cooking time. Many factors – type of fuel used, the weather, atmospheric pressure, wind speed – combine to make cooking to an exact time an impossible task. A thermometer will give you confidence.

When cooking meat, remove it from the grill when it's 5–8°C (9–14°F) below serving temperature, then let it rest. Resting it for 10 minutes is important to let the fibres relax, which increases tenderness. As it rests, the internal temperature will continue to rise. Serving temperature guidelines for red meats (beef and lamb) are as follows: rare = 52°C (125°F); medium = 60°C (140°F); well done = 71°C (160°F). Chicken should be served at at least 74°C (165°F) when tested in the thickest part or the thigh. For pork, the internal temperature, near the bone, shoud read 63°C (145°F) for medium or 71°C (160°F) for well done.

Long-handled tongs

It's going to get hot in there! Long-handled metal tongs are ideal for turning food safely and quickly. My favourite type is flat on the bottom and has a tong on top, which makes flipping food a breeze.

Thick gloves or heatproof mitts

Long, preferably leather, gloves that protect your hands and forearms will let you safely work close to the grill without fear of burning.

Chapa or plancha

A heavy-duty flat surface you put on your grill bars to cook on. It allows you to easily cook things such as pancakes, or delicate foods such as fish.

Tins and pans

It's great to have roasting tins and frying pans (skillets) that you can use directly on the grill bars. They must be fireproof – so no plastic or wooden handles, and avoid anything with a nonstick surface. My favourites are made of heavy-duty spun iron, or cheap-and-cheerful enamel-covered metal. Using a variety of tins and pans will allow you to cook more adventurously, such as finishing off dishes in sauces, grilling small and delicate food – or even cooking a cake.

Fish cage

A hinged metal cage of two halves that can enclose fish fillets, fish skewers or a whole fish, inside. Using one of these will make turning delicate fish really straightforward. It will also make fish a lot less prone to sticking.

Wire brush

A wire brush is the very best thing to clean your grill with. Simply fire up your grill, and once it is good and hot give it a really thorough scrub.

Metal skewers

I recommend using metal skewers for cooking kebabs rather than wooden ones. They are infinitely reusable, and the metal helpfully conducts the heat through to the centre of your food, so it cooks more efficiently and evenly. They are easy to find in supermarkets during the summer months or online all year round.

Metal cloche

A metal dome that you place over food to create an extra-steamy lid for cooking under. It's a great piece of equipment for making the 'smash' burgers (see page 65). You can also improvise by upending a large metal mixing bowl.

Silicone pastry brushes

For adding glazes and basting during cooking; something long-handled is best.

ESSENTIAL TECHNIQUES

Direct vs indirect cooking

The most important technique to master is an understanding of how to set up different heat zones on your barbecue. For indirect cooking, put lit charcoal on one half of the barbecue and leave the the other half empty. This allows you to cook on two zones: directly (over the fire) and indirectly (off the fire), and in between for moderate heat. Control the temperature by moving food closer to or further away from the heat source. For recipes that call for 'direct cooking', you also put the lit charcoal to one side of the barbecue, then you cook directly over the fire, but can easily slide food further away if its cooking too fast.

Never flood the base of your grill with charcoal – once it is alight you will have nowhere to hide if the heat becomes too fierce. Unless otherwise specified in the recipes, cook with the barbecue lid down. Doing so will hugely increase the energy efficiency and speed of cooking.

Dealing with flare-ups

Even with the best-laid plans for heat control, you occasionally get it wrong. If you suddenly have flames raging around your barbecue, you have a flare-up on your hands. Flare-ups are caused by excessively fatty foods being too close to the fire, or by greasy grill bars from previous cooks. The best thing to do is remove the food from the grill and wait for the flames to subside. Brushing the grills with a wire brush helps, as does cooking fatty foods slightly indirectly.

Rescuing a sulking fire

Conversely, a fire can sulk. Damp fuel, wet weather, or a lack of air circulating around the charcoal can all be causes. The best thing to do is inject a bit of oxygen into the fire. You can buy special metal blowpipes for this purpose but I find that a length of copper water pipe, slightly flattened at the fire end, works just as well.

CHICKEN

Quite possibly the nation's favourite meat, you can't go wrong with chicken on the barbecue. In most cases it is better to cook chicken more gently for a longer time than to try and rush it over a high heat, so be sure to master the direct vs indirect cooking technique. It is probably your most important barbecue skill! By cooking more gently you keep things juicy and make sure you cook it thoroughly without drying the meat or burning the outside. A temperature probe is very useful for cooking chicken to give you confidence that it's cooked safely.

SPATCHCOCK CHICKEN WITH COCONUT & SOY

Spatchcocking – flattening out a whole bird by removing its backbone – is a great way to barbecue a whole chicken because the meat cooks quickly and evenly.

2kg (4lb 8oz) free-range chicken
1 tbsp olive oil
sea salt and freshly ground
   black pepper

For the baste
½ × 400g (14fl oz) can coconut
   milk (freeze the rest)
1 garlic clove, finely chopped
2 tbsp soft brown sugar
2 tbsp soy sauce
1 tbsp fish sauce
zest and juice of 1 lime

To serve
a few sprigs of mint, chopped
2 red chillies, chopped (optional)

On a chopping board, use a sharp knife to make a few deep slashes through the meat, on both the breast and legs (this helps the heat penetrate to the middle more quickly). Turn the bird breast-side down on the chopping board and, using heavy-duty kitchen scissors, cut down each side of the backbone. Remove and discard. Turn the bird breast-side up and press down firmly to open it out flat.

Fire up the barbecue ready for direct and indirect cooking (see page 9).

Drizzle the chicken with the olive oil and season well with salt and freshly ground black pepper. Lay onto the grill bars, away from the heat source, skin-side up. Rest a heavy object on top to weigh it down; a chapa (see page 8) is ideal, or use a heavy frying pan (skillet). Shut the lid. Leave to cook for 45 minutes, checking once or twice and rotating the chicken to make sure it cooks evenly, but leave skin-side up.

Make a baste by stirring together the coconut milk, garlic, brown sugar, soy sauce, fish sauce and the lime zest in a bowl. Reserve the lime for squeezing the juice over the chicken once cooked.

Once the chicken has had 45 minutes skin-side up, turn it over and cook for a further 10 minutes skin-side down with the lid down. Use tongs to slide it directly over the fire and begin to brush with the baste, using a silicone pastry brush. Keep basting and turning for another 10–15 minutes until the chicken is deeply golden and cooked through. The temperature on a digital probe thermometer should read 74°C (165°F).

Lift the chicken onto a serving board then use a large knife to chop it into pieces. Squeeze over the reserved lime juice and scatter on the mint and chillies, if using.

Serves 4–6

–

Direct +
Indirect
Cooking

CHICKEN BURGERS WITH GRILLED PEPPERS & LEMON MAYO

I prefer to use chicken thigh fillets because they have more flavour, but do use breast if you prefer a leaner cut.

700g (1lb 9oz) chicken thigh fillets
2 tbsp olive oil
2 garlic cloves, finely chopped
1 tbsp dried mixed herbs
4 Romano peppers (the long red ones)
sea salt and freshly ground black
   pepper

For the lemon & chive mayo
zest and juice of 1 lemon
4 generous tbsp mayonnaise
a small bunch of chives, finely chopped

To serve
4 ciabatta rolls
a few extra chives, snipped, to garnish

For the lemon and chive mayo, grate the lemon zest into a small mixing bowl. Add the mayonnaise and chives, mix well, and season to taste with salt and pepper. Chill in the fridge.

Slash the chicken thighs deeply, but not all the way through (this will help the marinade to penetrate) then put in a bowl. Squeeze over the lemon juice, add the olive oil, garlic and herbs and season with salt and black pepper. Toss well to mix then cover and put in the fridge to marinate for 2 hours, or up to 12 hours if you like.

When you are ready to cook, fire up the barbecue ready for direct and indirect cooking (see page 9).

Arrange the chicken pieces over the unlit side of the barbecue and cook indirectly with the lid down for about 20 minutes, depending on the thickness of the fillets. Turn over occasionally so they cook and crisp evenly. Use a knife to cut one open at the thickest part to check it is cooked through. Using a digital probe thermometer, the internal temperature should be 74°C (165°F).

At the same time you start to cook the chicken, lay the whole peppers onto the grill over the fire so they cook over direct heat, turning occasionally until they are lightly chargrilled and soft.

Once the chicken and peppers are cooked, move everything off the heat. Open up the rolls and lay them cut-side down over the fire to toast for a minute or so.

To serve, put a couple of pieces of chicken into each roll and top with a whole pepper. Add a dollop of the lemon and chive mayo, sprinkle over the chives and tuck in while hot.

Serves 4
–
Direct +
Indirect
Cooking

VIETNAMESE CHICKEN WITH LIME LEAF BUTTER

Fresh lime leaves can be a little tricky to find, so substitute with a handful of coriander if you struggle to track them down.

700g (1lb 9oz) chicken thigh fillets
1 tbsp vegetable oil
juice of 1 lime
1 tbsp fish sauce
2 tsp soft brown sugar
1 banana shallot, finely chopped
   (or 2 round shallots)
2 garlic cloves, finely chopped
2–3 bird's eye chillies, chopped
½ tsp Chinese five-spice
sea salt and freshly ground black
   pepper

For the lime leaf butter
75g (⅓ cup) unsalted
   butter, softened
6 fresh lime leaves, finely chopped
a good pinch of sea salt flakes

To serve
6 mini rolls, or 1 large loaf, sliced
a handful of soft lettuce leaves
1 slightly underripe mango, sliced
a little extra chopped chilli, to garnish
   (optional)

Slash the chicken fillets deeply but not all the way through a few times (this will help the marinade to penetrate). Transfer to a bowl and add the vegetable oil, lime juice, fish sauce, brown sugar, shallot, garlic, chillies and five-spice. Season with salt and pepper and stir well until the chicken is evenly coated. Cover and refrigerate for 1–2 hours.

While the chicken is marinating, make the lime leaf butter by mashing together the softened butter, lime leaves and sea salt flakes in a bowl. Set aside.

When you are ready to cook, fire up the barbecue ready for direct and indirect cooking (see page 9).

Arrange the fillets on the grill bars, away from the fire so they cook indirectly. Cook for about 20 minutes with the lid down, turning and rotating the fillets a few times so they cook evenly and brushing with the leftover marinade as you go. Use a knife to cut one open at the thickest part to check it is cooked through. Using a digital probe thermometer, the internal temperature should be 74°C (165°F).

Once the chicken is cooked, pile it up on one side of the grill, away from the fire, and rest the rolls onto the grill bars to warm through for a couple of minutes.

To serve, slice the warm rolls through the centre and add a few lettuce leaves and mango slices. Add a couple of pieces of the hot chicken and then top with a good spoonful of the butter and a sprinkle of extra chilli if you like. Squeeze the roll shut and allow the butter to melt for a few seconds before tucking in.

Serves 4–6
–
Direct +
Indirect
Cooking

CHICKEN LEGS WITH ALABAMA WHITE SAUCE

This creamy sauce is quite spicy with horseradish, pepper and chilli. You can reduce the quantities of each if you prefer less heat, but its beauty lies in its punchiness.

6 chicken legs
2 thick slices good bread, cubed
3 tbsp olive oil
3 garlic cloves
a couple of sprigs of rosemary
6 vine tomatoes, halved
2 × 80g (2¾oz) bags watercress
sea salt and freshly ground black
    pepper

For the Alabama white sauce
200ml (scant 1 cup) mayonnaise
100ml (7 tbsp) cider vinegar
juice of ½ lemon
2 tbsp hot horseradish sauce
1 tbsp black peppercorns, crushed
1 tsp chilli flakes (optional)

Fire up the barbecue ready for direct and indirect cooking (see page 9).

Make a few deep slashes in the meat of each chicken leg and season with salt and pepper. Set onto the grill bars away from the fire and leave to cook indirectly, with the lid down, for a good 20 minutes, turning and rotating once or twice.

While the chicken is cooking, make the sauce by whisking together the mayonnaise, vinegar, lemon juice, horseradish, crushed peppercorns and chilli flakes in a bowl. Season to taste with salt. Transfer half to a small serving bowl to use as a dressing for the finished dish. Take the other half to the barbecue and have a silicone pastry brush ready for basting.

Tip the bread cubes into a fireproof pan (no wooden or plastic handles) and drizzle over 2 tbsp of the olive oil. Use the flat of a large knife to bruise the garlic cloves and add them to the pan with the rosemary. Season with salt and pepper. Drizzle the remaining 1 tbsp olive oil onto the tomato halves and season with salt and pepper.

Once the chicken has had its 20 minutes' cooking time, begin basting with the sauce. Brush all over regularly and keep cooking and turning for a further 20 minutes, or until the chicken is cooked through. When tested with a digital probe thermometer in the thickest part of the leg, it should read 74°C (165°F).

When you start basting the chicken, set the pan of bread over the direct fire and cook until crisp and golden, tossing to cook evenly. Remove the croutons from the fire and set aside. At the same time, rest the tomato halves over the fire so they grill and soften, turning to cook both sides.

To serve, scatter the watercress onto a large platter and top with the grilled tomatoes. Add the chicken legs and sprinkle over the croutons. Drizzle with some of the reserved sauce and serve the rest alongside.

Serves 6

–

**Direct +
Indirect
Cooking**

CHICKEN YAKITORI WITH CARROT & SESAME SLAW

Tare sauce is the sticky glaze that gives these skewers their flavour. The sauce can burn quite easily, so watch the skewers as they cook and slide them away from the heat if necessary.

700g (1lb 9oz) chicken thigh fillets, cut into 3cm (1¼in) cubes
1 bunch of spring onions (scallions), trimmed and sliced into 3cm (1¼in) lengths
1 tbsp vegetable oil

For the tare sauce
7 tbsp soy sauce
7 tbsp mirin
7 tbsp sake
1cm (½in) piece of fresh root ginger, finely grated
2 tsp soft brown sugar

For the slaw
1 red pepper, cut into matchsticks
3 carrots, cut into matchsticks
3 spring onions (scallions), sliced
2 tbsp sesame seeds, toasted
2 tbsp sesame oil
2 tbsp rice vinegar
sea salt and freshly ground black pepper

You will also need 6 long metal skewers.

For the sauce, put the ingredients into a small saucepan set over a medium-low heat on the hob (stovetop) and bring to the boil. Allow to simmer steadily until reduced in volume by half (15–20 minutes). Divide between 2 small dishes and set aside to cool. One dish will be used as a dipping sauce, the other to glaze the skewers as they cook. Separating them prevents cross-contamination from the raw meat.

Make the slaw by stirring together the red pepper, carrot and spring onions (scallions) with the sesame seeds, sesame oil and rice vinegar. Season to taste with salt and pepper.

Alternately thread the chicken pieces and sliced spring onions onto the skewers and drizzle all over with the 1 tbsp vegetable oil.

Light the barbecue and set up the fire for direct cooking (see page 9).

Rest the skewers on the grill bars over the fire. Take one of the bowls of sauce and, using a silicone pastry brush, glaze the chicken all over. Lower the lid. After 2–3 minutes turn the skewers and brush over more sauce. Keep turning and brushing the chicken with sauce until cooked through (10–12 minutes, depending on thickness).

Serve the skewers with the slaw and the other dish of sauce for dipping into.

DEVILLED CHICKEN WINGS WITH SPICY TOMATO RELISH

These Sri Lankan-inspired wings are deliciously spicy and rather addictive. You could use thighs instead, in which case increase the cooking time by 15 minutes or so.

1kg (2lb 4oz) chicken wings
2 tbsp red wine vinegar
1 tbsp vegetable oil
3 garlic cloves, finely chopped
a thumb-sized piece of fresh root
    ginger, grated
2 tsp chilli flakes
2 tsp black peppercorns, crushed
1 tsp ground turmeric
1 tsp salt

For the relish
1 onion, chopped
1 tbsp vegetable oil
2 garlic cloves, finely chopped
1 tsp cumin seeds, crushed
1 tsp coriander seeds, crushed
1 tsp ground turmeric
1 tsp chilli flakes
1 tsp mustard seeds
400g (14oz) ripe tomatoes, chopped
a small bunch of coriander (cilantro),
    chopped
sea salt and freshly ground
    black pepper

Put the chicken wings in a glass or ceramic bowl and add the vinegar, oil, garlic, ginger, chilli flakes, peppercorns, turmeric and salt. Stir together until the wings are evenly coated. Cover and refrigerate for 2–3 hours, or overnight if you have time.

When you are ready to cook, fire up the barbecue ready for direct and indirect cooking (see page 9).

Lay the chicken wings onto the grill bars, away from the fire so they cook gently. Leave to cook with the lid down for 30–40 minutes, turning every now and then until they are crisp and cooked through. The temperature when tested with a digital probe thermometer should read 74°C (165°F).

Meanwhile, for the relish, set a small fireproof pan over the fire then add the onion and vegetable oil. Fry until the onion is softened and lightly caramelized then add the garlic, cumin seeds, coriander seeds, turmeric and chilli flakes. Fry for a further 2–3 minutes, then add the tomatoes and chopped coriander (cilantro).

Leave to simmer and soften over the fire while the chicken is cooking. Once the relish has thickened, transfer to a serving bowl and set aside to cool to room temperature.

Serve the wings hot from the grill with the relish alongside to spoon over or dip into as you eat.

Serves 4–6
as a snack
–
Direct +
Indirect
Cooking

HERBY CHICKEN BREASTS & MELTING POTATOES

Don't be tempted to stint on the butter – it's what gives the potatoes their melting texture.

4 chicken breasts, skin on
2 tbsp balsamic vinegar
1 tbsp olive oil
4 garlic cloves, finely chopped
2 tsp dried mixed herbs
1 kg (2lb 4oz) potatoes, peeled and
    sliced in 5mm (¼in) discs
300ml (1¼ cups) vegetable
    or chicken stock
75g (⅓ cup) butter, cut into
    1cm (½in) cubes
sea salt and freshly ground
    black pepper

Lay the chicken breasts on a chopping board and use a sharp knife to cut a few deep slashes through the skin and into the meat (this will help the marinade to penetrate the meat). Lay the breasts in a shallow glass or ceramic bowl and pour over the balsamic vinegar and oil. Add half the garlic and the herbs and season with salt and pepper, tossing to coat the chicken all over. Cover and put in the fridge for 2–3 hours, or up to 1 day, to marinate.

When you are ready to cook, fire up the barbecue ready for direct and indirect cooking (see page 9).

Tip the potato slices into a large fireproof pan or old roasting tin. Stir in the garlic and a good grind of salt and pepper. Pour in the stock, pressing the potatoes down into it as much as possible and dot the top with the butter. Rest the roasting tin on the grill bars on the opposite side from the fire and cook indirectly for about 30 minutes with the lid down, until the potato slices are just tender. Slide the pan over the direct heat, once again shutting the lid on the barbecue. Leave to bubble away until most of the stock has been absorbed, then slide back off the heat to keep warm.

Once the potatoes are cooked, remove the chicken breasts from the marinade and place skin-side down on the grill bars directly over the fire. Cook for a few minutes until the skin is golden brown, then turn and cook on the other side. Once the chicken has a good colour, slide off the heat and cook indirectly for another few minutes. Use a digital probe thermometer to test the thickest part of the breast. It should read 74°C (165°F). Depending on the size, they should take about 15 minutes in total.

When everything is cooked, spoon the potatoes onto warmed plates. Slice the chicken and rest on top of the potatoes. Serve with a simple green salad.

Serves 4

–

**Direct +
Indirect
Cooking**

TANDOORI CHICKEN SKEWERS

These are prone to sticking, so clean the grill bars with a wire brush before you start. If they start to catch and burn, slide them a little away from the heat to cook more gently.

1 tbsp cumin seeds
1 tbsp coriander seeds
1 tbsp paprika (unsmoked)
1–2 tsp chilli flakes, to taste
1 tsp ground turmeric
1 tsp ground cinnamon
150g (½ cup) full fat yogurt
50g (1¾oz) fresh root ginger, grated
2 garlic cloves, finely chopped
4 skinless chicken breasts
6 vine tomatoes, sliced
1 red onion, sliced
sea salt and freshly ground
    black pepper
juice of 1 lemon
a handful of coriander (cilantro),
    chopped

To serve
naan bread (or similar flatbread)
mango chutney (or other chutney of
    your choice)

You will also need 4–6 long metal skewers.

Put the cumin and coriander seeds in a small frying pan (skillet) set over a medium heat on the hob (stovetop) and toast for a couple of minutes. Transfer to a pestle and mortar, add the paprika, chilli flakes, turmeric and cinnamon and grind to a coarse powder. Transfer to a shallow dish, add the yogurt, ginger, garlic and some salt and pepper, stirring well to mix.

Slice the chicken breasts lengthways into long strips, adding them to the marinade as you go. Toss well to coat, then cover and marinate for 2–3 hours in the fridge, or up to 1 day if you have time.

When you are ready to cook, light the barbecue and set up the fire for direct cooking (see page 9).

Thread the marinated chicken strips onto the skewers, wrapping and piercing them several times so they're secure.

When the barbecue is hot, clean the grill bars using a wire brush to minimize sticking. Lay the skewers on the grill over the fire and cook for 10–12 minutes with the lid down, turning a couple of times, until they are cooked through. The temperature when tested with a digital probe thermometer should read 74°C (165°F).

To serve, scatter the tomatoes and onion over 4 plates and season with salt and pepper. Top each with a skewer, then squeeze over the lemon juice and sprinkle on the chopped coriander (cilantro).

Serve with naan bread, warmed on the grill for 2–3 minutes, and the mango chutney.

Serves 4–6
–
Direct
Cooking

CIDER CAN CHICKEN WITH ONION & THYME GRAVY

Cooking the chicken with the cider results in super-moist meat because it adds steam to the cooking process and as a bonus you get to make a delicious gravy once the chicken is cooked.

2kg (4lb 8oz) free-range chicken
2 tbsp olive oil
440ml (15fl oz) can (hard) cider
2 large onions, sliced
50g (4 tbsp) butter, cubed
3–4 sprigs of thyme
2 garlic cloves, finely chopped
1 heaped tbsp cornflour (cornstarch),
    mixed with 1 tbsp cold water
salt and freshly ground black pepper

Fire up the barbecue ready for indirect cooking (see page 9). If you are using a chimney starter (see page 7) fill it halfway with good charcoal. Once lit, tip it in a little heap on one side of the barbecue. For an extra-smoky chicken, add a lump of smoking wood to the top of the fire.

Drizzle the chicken with the olive oil and season all over with salt and pepper. Pour one third of the cider into a jug or bowl and set aside. Take the chicken and lower it onto the cider can, pushing the can deep into the cavity so the chicken looks like it's sitting upright with its legs pointing downwards. Lift into the centre of a fireproof roasting tin.

Scatter the onions around the chicken, dot with the butter and tuck in the thyme sprigs.

Carefully lift the roasting tin onto the barbecue grill, making sure it's positioned as far away from the fire as possible and that the chicken is stable and upright. Shut the lid and leave to roast gently for 2–2½ hours. Halfway through cooking, pour the cider from the jug/bowl into the roasting tin.

Every 30 minutes or so, rotate the tin a little to make sure it is cooking evenly and give the onions a little stir. Towards the end of cooking, use a digital probe termometer to test the chicken in the thickest part of the thigh. It should read a minimum of 74°C (165°F) but chicken legs often benefit from cooking a little more, up to 80°C (176°F). It will stay good and moist because of the cider.

When the chicken is cooked, carefully lift it off the can of cider and onto a warmed plate. Cover loosely with foil to rest while you finish the gravy. Rest the roasting tin over a high heat on the hob (stovetop) and pour in the cider left in the can. Bring up to a brisk boil then whisk in the cornflour (cornstarch) paste to thicken, simmering for 5 minutes, or longer for a thicker gravy, then serve.

Serves 4–6
–
Indirect
Cooking

PORK

Pork is such a versatile meat for the barbecue, ready to take on all sorts of delicious flavours from spices and herbs. Some cuts, like fillet, are very lean, while others are rather more succulent and fatty. As a general rule of thumb, the more fat, the more likely you should be cooking indirectly away from the fire, while leaner meat can take more of a hot, direct heat.

PORK, APPLE & MUSTARD KEBABS

Pork and apple is a classic combo. Any variety of sharp apple will do here, but red ones add a beautiful splash of colour.

600g (1lb 5oz) pork leg steaks
2 tbsp wholegrain mustard
1 tbsp olive oil
25g (1oz) fresh sage, leaves chopped
2 large eating (dessert) apples,
　　no need to peel
sea salt and freshly ground
　　black pepper

To serve
4–6 large flatbreads
a few mixed salad leaves
extra wholegrain mustard (optional)

You will also need 4–6 long metal skewers.

Cut the pork steaks into 3cm (1¼in) cubes, dropping them into a mixing bowl as you go. Add the mustard, olive oil, chopped sage (reserve some for the garnish) and a good grind of salt and pepper. Stir well to coat the meat in the marinade, cover, then transfer to the fridge to marinate for 2 hours, or overnight if you have time.

When you are ready to cook, light the barbecue and set up the fire for direct cooking (see page 9).

Chop the apples into quarters, remove the cores, then cut each piece in half – you should have 16 wedges. Add the apple to the pork and stir to coat in the marinade. Thread alternating pieces of pork and apple onto the skewers.

Once the barbecue is hot, lay the skewers onto the grill bars a little away from the fire – you want to cook over a moderate heat. Shut the lid and cook for 20 minutes, or until the pork is cooked through; the internal temperature should read 63°C (145°F) for medium or 71°C (160°F) for well done on a digital thermometer.

Scatter over the reserved chopped sage, and serve with the flatbreads, salad leaves and mustard on the side if you like.

Serves 4–6
–
Direct Cooking

MEXICAN PORK BURGER WRAPS WITH AVOCADO & SOUR CREAM

These are a little messy to eat but that's half the fun. Pack the wraps generously with all the extras and have plenty of paper towels on hand.

2 tsp cumin seeds
500g (1lb 2oz) pork mince
     (ground pork)
3 spring onions (scallions),
     finely chopped
a handful of coriander (cilantro),
     finely chopped
2 garlic cloves, finely chopped
1 tsp dried chilli flakes, or to taste
sea salt and freshly ground black
     pepper
a little olive oil, for drizzling

To serve
4 large soft tortilla wraps, snugly
     wrapped in a foil parcel
4 tbsp sour cream
2 large ripe avocados, sliced
2 large vine tomatoes, sliced
a handful of grated mature Cheddar
a small bunch of coriander (cilantro),
     chopped
a few drops of hot chilli sauce,
     to taste (optional)

Toast the cumin seeds in a small frying pan (skillet) over a medium heat for a minute on the hob (stovetop), then tip into a mixing bowl. Add the pork mince (ground pork), spring onions (scallions), coriander (cilantro), garlic and chilli flakes, then season with salt and pepper. Mix thoroughly, then shape into 8 equal balls, flattening each into a little burger.

When you are ready to cook, fire up the barbecue ready for direct cooking (see page 9). Pork mince tends to stick, so get the grill bars nice and hot and then give them a scrub with a wire brush so they are squeaky clean.

Drizzle a little oil over each of the burgers and lay directly onto the grill bars over the fire and cook with the lid down for about 5 minutes. Test by raising a corner of one of the burgers. If it is stuck to the grill, leave for another minute. As it develops a delicious golden crust it will free itself from the grill. Turn the burgers and cook for a further 5 minutes, or until cooked through.

Once the burgers are nearly cooked, put the foil parcel of tortillas onto the grill bars and allow the tortillas to warm through for a couple of minutes.

To serve, spread a little sour cream over each tortilla, top with the avocado and tomato and sprinkle over the cheese. Add two mini burgers to each wrap and sprinkle over the coriander and hot sauce, if using. Wrap each up, tucking in the ends so the filling is secure, and eat while hot.

Serves 4
–
Direct
Cooking

Pork

PORK BELLY WITH FENNEL & APPLE SLAW

Pork belly benefits from long, slow cooking, so don't be tempted to rush it over a higher heat. Slow, indirect cooking will guarantee succulence.

2 tsp caraway seeds
1–2 tsp chipotle chilli flakes, to taste
2 garlic cloves, roughly chopped
2 tsp dark soft brown sugar
1 tbsp olive oil
250ml (generous 1 cup) dark beer
1.5kg (3lb 5oz) pork belly,
    cut into thick slices
sea salt and freshly ground
    black pepper

For the slaw

2 fennel bulbs, finely shredded
    (reserve a few chopped fronds
    to serve)
2 eating (dessert) apples,
    finely chopped
½ bunch of spring onions (scallions),
    thinly sliced
a small bunch of tarragon,
    leaves chopped
2 tbsp mayonnaise
2 tbsp natural yogurt
juice of 1 lemon

Roughly grind the caraway seeds in a pestle and mortar. Add the chipotle flakes, garlic, brown sugar and olive oil, season with salt and pepper, then mix to a paste. Transfer to a food bag, sit inside a bowl to keep it open, and pour in the beer. Add the pork belly slices and seal tightly, squeezing out as much air as possible, and turning the bag over a few times to mix everything together. Transfer to the fridge to marinate for up to 24 hours (the longer the better for maximum flavour).

When you are ready to cook, light the barbecue and set up the fire for indirect cooking (see page 9). Add a few lumps of smoking wood for some extra smoky flavour (see page 7).

Lift the pork from the marinade (reserve the marinade) using tongs and lay the slices snugly together on the grill bars furthest from the heat. Shut the lid and cook over indirect heat for about 3 hours. Every 30 minutes, lift the lid and brush the pork with the marinade, turning over the slices as you go. Add a couple of lumps of charcoal every 30 minutes to keep the temperature low and steady.

While the pork is slowly cooking, make the slaw. Stir together the fennel, apple, spring onions (scallions) and tarragon in a mixing bowl. Add the mayonnaise, yogurt and lemon juice then season to taste with salt and freshly ground black pepper. Cover and refrigerate until the pork is ready.

Serve the pork hot and juicy straight from the grill with the slaw on the side, scattered with the chopped fennel fronds.

Serves 4–6
–
Indirect
Cooking

LEMON & OREGANO SOUVLAKI WITH TZATZIKI

This dish is packed full of sunshine flavours. Cooking the pork in one large kebab for slicing and sharing keeps the meat nice and juicy.

3 tbsp olive oil
zest and juice of 2 lemons
3 garlic cloves, finely chopped
a small bunch of fresh oregano, chopped (or 1 tbsp dried oregano)
1kg (2lb 4oz) pork leg steaks
sea salt and freshly ground black pepper

For the tzatziki
300ml (1¼ cups) Greek yogurt
½ cucumber, grated
a small bunch of mint, chopped, plus extra to garnish
1 garlic clove, finely chopped
2 tbsp extra virgin olive oil

To serve
baby salad leaves
4–6 pitta breads, toasted

You will also need 6 long metal skewers.

Use a large roasting tin that will fit the pork steaks in a single layer. Pour in the olive oil, add the zest of both lemons and the juice of one lemon, the garlic and the oregano, along with a good grind of salt and pepper. Add the pork, turning the steaks over a few times in the marinade. Cover and transfer to the fridge to marinate for 2 hours, turning the pork another 2 or 3 times if you can.

While the meat is marinating, make the tzatziki. Mix the yogurt, cucumber, mint and garlic together in a bowl. Season to taste with salt and pepper then spoon into a serving dish and refrigerate until required.

When you are ready to cook, light the barbecue and set up the fire for indirect cooking (see page 9).

Lift the pork steaks from the marinade (reserve for basting), and lay one on top of the other in a vertical stack on a chopping board. Pierce the skewers down through the stack, evenly spaced around the meat, to pin the steaks together in a secure, neat pile. (You can dice the steaks into cubes and thread onto skewers if you prefer.)

Rest the meat onto the grill bars as far away from the fire as possible and shut the lid. Leave to cook gently for 1 hour 15 minutes. It is ready when the internal temperature reads 63°C (145°F) for medium or 71°C (160°F) for well done. Every 15–20 minutes, lift the lid, rotate the joint and brush over a little of the marinade.

To serve, transfer the meat to a clean chopping board and pull out the skewers. Squeeze over the juice of the reserved lemon and scatter over the mint. Slice the meat into strips and serve with the tzatziki, salad and toasted pitta bread.

Serves 4–6
–
Indirect Cooking

PIGS IN BLANKETS, HONEY & MUSTARD

The easiest and most delicious thing to do with a pack of sausages. Skewering the sausages together makes for super-easy turning and basting in the sticky glaze.

12 chipolatas (small pork sausages, such as breakfast sausage)
12 slices smoked streaky bacon
2 tbsp runny honey
1–2 tbsp mustard (Dijon or wholegrain)
a little olive oil, to drizzle
sea salt flakes, to serve

You will also need 3 long metal skewers.

Fire up the barbecue ready for direct cooking (see page 9).

Wrap each sausage snugly in a slice of bacon and line them up on a chopping board. Pierce one metal skewer through each sausage about 1cm (½in) from the end, so they are all attached. Thread another skewer through all the sausages at the other end. Thread the third skewer through the middle to secure in one neat slab.

Mix the honey and mustard in a small bowl and take to the barbecue, along with a silicone pastry brush for basting.

Once the barbecue is hot, drizzle a little olive oil over the sausages and rest on the grill bars, you want to cook them over a moderate heat, slightly away from the fire so they don't cook too quickly. Cook for 10 minutes with the lid down, lifting it to turn and rotate the skewers 2 or 3 times so they cook evenly.

After 10 minutes, brush the sausages all over with the honey and mustard glaze. Cook for a further 10 minutes, turning regularly, until they are sticky and golden.

To serve, grab the ends of the skewers, using a mitt to protect your hands, and twist and pull out the skewers. Scatter with sea salt flakes and eat while hot.

Serves 4
as a snack
–
Direct
Cooking

Pork

SMOKY PORK, ASPARAGUS & SPRING ONION SKEWERS

Pork fillet cooks quickly, so it's ideal paired with asparagus, which takes no time to char to perfection. Threading the meat and vegetables onto a double skewer keeps everything secure and makes turning easy.

500g (1lb 2oz) pork fillet (tenderloin)
1 garlic clove, finely chopped
1–2 tsp smoked paprika, to taste
3 tbsp olive oil
1 tbsp sherry vinegar
250g (9oz) asparagus, trimmed
    and sliced into thirds
1 bunch of spring onions (scallions),
    trimmed and sliced into thirds
a little flat-leaf parsley, chopped,
    to garnish
sea salt and freshly ground
    black pepper

You will also need 6 long metal skewers.

Use a sharp knife to trim away any fat and membrane from the pork. Cut across the grain into 5mm (¼in) thick slices, dropping them into a bowl as you go. Add the garlic, smoked paprika, olive oil and sherry vinegar, then stir well to mix. Cover and refrigerate for 1–2 hours, then stir in the asparagus and spring onions (scallions) to coat in the seasoned oil.

Take a skewer and alternately thread pieces of pork, asparagus and spring onion onto it, piercing the skewer through at one end of each piece. Once the skewer is full, thread a second skewer carefully through at the other end, so you end up with two skewers, one down each side. Repeat twice more to make three double skewers.

Fire up the barbecue ready for direct cooking (see page 9).

Set the skewers directly onto the grill bars over the fire and cook for 10 minutes, turning and rotating 1 or 2 times so they cook evenly.

Sprinkle over a little chopped parsley before serving.

Serves 4
–
Direct
Cooking

PORK, FENNEL & LEMON BURGERS WITH GRILLED AUBERGINE

Soaking breadcrumbs in milk is an Italian trick that helps keep pork mince tender. They can be a little delicate on the grill but chilling them before cooking helps hold them together.

100g (1 cup) fresh breadcrumbs
50ml (3 tbsp) milk
500g (1lb 2oz) pork mince
  (ground pork)
50g (3½oz) Parmesan, grated
1 egg
finely grated zest of 1 lemon
1 garlic clove, finely chopped
2 tsp fennel seeds, ground
a small bunch of flat-leaf parsley,
  chopped
1 large aubergine (eggplant), cut
  into 1.5cm (⅝in) thick discs
2 tbsp olive oil, plus a little extra
  for brushing
sea salt and freshly ground black
  pepper

To serve
4 ciabatta rolls, sliced open
a generous handful of rocket
  (arugula) leaves
tomato relish or chilli ketchup
  (optional)

Put the breadcrumbs into a mixing bowl, pour over the milk, then leave to soak for 10 minutes until the milk is absorbed. Add the pork mince (ground pork), Parmesan, egg, lemon zest, garlic, ground fennel seeds, parsley and a generous seasoning of salt and pepper. Mix with your hands until evenly combined then shape into 4 even-sized burgers. Chill in the fridge for 1 hour to firm up, or leave for up to 24 hours if you like.

When you are ready to cook, take the burgers from the fridge and brush on both sides with the olive oil. Fire up the barbecue ready for direct cooking (see page 9). When hot, put the burgers on the grill bars, lower the lid and cook for 8 minutes on each side.

Pork mince is prone to sticking. Test the burgers are ready by sliding a metal spatula under a corner of one burger. If it comes away easily from the grill and has a deep caramelized crust, it's ready to turn. If it's stuck, leave it for a further minute or two before turning, then grill until cooked through.

Once the burgers are on the grill, brush the aubergine (eggplant) slices with a little extra oil, then lay them alongside the burgers to cook, turning them a few times until lightly charred and tender all the way through.

Toast the ciabatta rolls, cut-sides down, for a minute or two on the grill.

To serve, put some rocket (arugula) onto the base of the bun and top with a burger. Add a couple slices of aubergine, and top with a dollop of tomato relish or ketchup, if using, before adding the bun lid.

Serves 4
–
Direct
Cooking

Pork

PORK CHOPS WITH GRILLED RED CABBAGE & PORCINI BUTTER

Brining the meat first keeps the chops succulent and tender, and it's a really easy thing to do. Just make sure the brine is cold before you add the chops to it.

3 tbsp sea salt
1 tbsp soft brown sugar
1 tbsp juniper berries, crushed
a small bunch of sage, leaves finely shredded
4 × 200–250g (7–9oz) large bone-in pork chops
25g (1oz) dried porcini mushrooms
100g (7 tbsp) butter, softened
1 medium red cabbage, about 800g (1lb 12oz)
3 tbsp olive oil, plus extra for the chops
100g (1 cup) breadcrumbs
sea salt and freshly ground black pepper

Brine the pork chops 2–3 hours in advance (or the day before). Pour 400ml (1¾ cups) freshly boiled water into a heatproof jug. Stir in the salt, sugar, juniper berries and most of the sage (set some aside to garnish). Leave to go cold.

Once cold, place the chops in a large food bag and set it in a bowl to keep the top of the bag open. Pour in the brine, squeezing the bag to make sure the chops are submerged. Tie up the bag, squeeze out the air, transfer to the fridge and leave to brine for 2–3 hours, or overnight if possible.

Put the porcini in a heatproof bowl and pour over boiling water to cover. Set aside to soften for 10 minutes. Drain, (reserve the soaking water), finely chop, then stir into the softened butter. Season with salt and pepper and set aside.

Slice the cabbage into wedges through the root, drizzle with the 3 tbsp olive oil and season with salt and pepper.

Fire up the barbecue ready for direct and indirect cooking (see page 9).

Lay the cabbage wedges onto the grill bars directly over the fire, pour over the reserved porcini soaking water, lower the lid and cook for 5 minutes on each side until lightly charred and starting to soften. Transfer to a fireproof roasting tin and dot the wedges with the porcini butter. Sprinkle over the breadcrumbs and set the tin back onto the barbecue, away from the fire so that the butter melts into the cabbage and the breadcrumbs crisp up. Lower the lid.

Drain the chops from the brine, discarding the brine. Drizzle a little oil over the chops and lay on the grill bars directly over the fire. Cook for 5–6 minutes on each side until cooked through and caramelized. On a digital probe thermometer, the internal temperature near the bone should read 63°C (145°F) for medium or 71°C (160°F) for well done. To serve, rest the chops on the buttery cabbage and sprinkle over the reserved sage.

Serves 4
–
Direct +
Indirect
Cooking

JERK PORK STEAKS WITH PINEAPPLE SALSA

The jerk marinade is a little prone to sticking because of the sugar, so set up your grill for indirect and direct grilling. Once the steaks have taken on a good colour over direct heat, you can move them to indirect heat to cook more gently.

For the pork steaks

2cm (¾in) piece of fresh root ginger, finely grated
2 garlic cloves, finely chopped
1 Scotch bonnet chilli, finely chopped (seeds removed for less heat)
2 tbsp olive oil
2 tsp soft brown sugar
2 tsp ground allspice
1 tsp ground cinnamon
1 tsp paprika (unsmoked)
a few sprigs of fresh thyme, leaves picked and chopped, plus extra to garnish
6 × 150g (5½oz) pork shoulder steaks

For the pineapple salsa

½ fresh pineapple
3 shallots, finely chopped
a handful of coriander (cilantro), roughly chopped
3 red chillies, deseeded and chopped
zest and juice of 1 lime

Mix the ginger, garlic, Scotch bonnet, olive oil, sugar, allspice, cinnamon, paprika and thyme in a small bowl. Coat the pork steaks well with the paste, put on a plate, cover and refrigerate for 1–2 hours, longer if you have time. The pork will happily marinate for a day.

While the pork is marinating make the salsa. Use a large sharp knife to chop off the top and bottom of the pineapple, then slice down in thin strips to remove the peel. The pineapple will now be left with lots of unsightly brown eyes that you don't want to eat. You will see that the eyes are in spiral lines running diagonally around the pineapple.

Turn the pineapple on its side, take a small sharp knife and cut a deep V-shaped trench down either side of each row of eyes, removing the row in one piece. Rotate the pineapple and move onto the next row. Repeat until all the eyes are removed and then chop the pineapple finely.

Mix the pineapple, shallots, coriander (cilantro), chillies and lime juice and zest in a bowl. Leave to rest at room temperature to allow the flavours to develop.

When you are ready to cook, fire up the barbecue ready for direct and indirect cooking (see page 9).

Lay the pork steaks on the grill bars directly over the fire and cook for a couple of minutes each side with the lid down until nicely charred all over. Slide them over to the cooler side of the grill, lower the lid and cook more gently for another few minutes until cooked through. On a digital probe thermometer, the internal temperature near the bone should read 63°C (145°F) for medium or 71°C (160°F) for well done.

Scatter the extra thyme leaves over the pork and serve with the pineapple salsa on the side.

Serves 6
–
Direct +
Indirect
Cooking

STICKY BARBECUED PORK RIBS

If you have time, make the barbecue sauce a couple of days before you want to use it, to let the flavours mellow a little. It also stores really well – up to three months in the fridge – and goes brilliantly with all sorts of barbecued foods.

1kg (2lb 4oz) pork ribs (2 racks)
   (also called baby back ribs)
2 tbsp barbecue seasoning
250ml (1 generous cup)
   apple juice or cider
coleslaw, to serve (optional)

For the barbecue sauce (makes 2 jars)
1 tbsp vegetable oil
1 small onion, finely chopped
3 garlic cloves, finely chopped
300g (1½ cups) tomato ketchup
100ml (7 tbsp) cider vinegar
100g (5 tbsp) black treacle
   (blackstrap molasses)
3 tbsp soft brown sugar
3 tbsp Worcestershire sauce
3 tbsp English (hot yellow) mustard
1 tbsp hot smoked paprika
1 tsp salt

For the barbecue sauce, heat the oil in a small heavy-based saucepan over a medium-low heat on the hob (stovetop). Add the onion and cook gently, stirring occasionally, for 20 minutes, or until the onion is soft but not coloured. Stir in the garlic and cook for 2 minutes more. Add the ketchup, cider vinegar, treacle (blackstrap molasses), sugar, Worcestershire sauce, mustard, paprika and salt and simmer over a low heat for 30 minutes, stirring occasionally.

When the sauce has finished cooking, allow to cool a little, pour into a blender and whizz until smooth. You could use a stick blender in the pan but be careful of hot splatters. Spoon into sterilized jam jars. Store in the fridge and use within three months.

When you are ready to cook the ribs, fire up the barbecue ready for indirect cooking, adding 2–3 lumps of smoking wood to the fire (see page 9).

Rub the ribs all over with the barbecue seasoning then rest onto the grill bars as far away from the fire as possible. Shut the lid and cook gently for 1½ hours, lifting the lid to rotate and turn the ribs a couple of times as they cook.

Lift the racks onto separate sheets of foil, bringing up the sides around the ribs. Pour in the apple juice (or cider), then seal up into parcels. Wrap each in a second layer of foil to ensure they are well sealed. Rest, seam-side up, back on the barbecue away from the fire, lower the lid and cook for 1 hour further.

Carefully lift the ribs from the foil back onto the grill bars, away from the fire, and baste all over with some of the barbecue sauce. Cook for another 30 minutes or so (lid down), basting and turning frequently until the ribs are sticky and deeply caramelized.

Serve with extra barbecue sauce for dipping with coleslaw on the side, if you like.

Serves 4

–

Indirect
Cooking

BEEF

Not just limited to steak, beef is a great
choice for the barbecue. A meat thermometer
is really useful to make sure you don't
overcook it. Don't forget that meat keeps on
cooking once you take it off the grill, so as
a general rule remove it to rest about 5°C
(9°F) below the ideal eating temperature.

LEMONGRASS BEEF SKEWERS

Skirt beef is a really lean cut that cooks quickly over a hot, direct heat. Due to the high heat, metal skewers are recommended as wooden ones often burn, even if you soak them in water.

600g (1lb 5oz) skirt steak
  (flank steak)
2 lemongrass stalks
1 tbsp black peppercorns, crushed
2 banana shallots, very finely chopped
3 garlic cloves, finely chopped
2 tsp caster (superfine) sugar
3 tbsp fish sauce
1 tbsp vegetable oil
2 limes, halved

To serve
cooked egg noodles,
  tossed in sesame oil
1 bunch of spring onions (scallions),
  thinly sliced
a handful of coriander (cilantro),
  chopped
3–4 bird's eye chillies, finely chopped,
  to taste

You will also need 4 metal skewers.

Begin by wrapping the beef in baking parchment and freezing it for 2 hours. Briefly freezing the meat will firm it up and make it easier to slice thinly.

While the beef is in the freezer, make the marinade. Discard the outer leaves of the lemongrass stalks and very finely chop the inner core. Put in a bowl with the crushed peppercorns, shallots, garlic, caster (superfine) sugar, fish sauce and vegetable oil and mix well. Set aside.

Take the beef out of the freezer and unwrap. Use a really sharp knife to cut into 3mm (⅛in) slices, cutting across the grain. Add the beef to the marinade and mix thoroughly to coat the meat. Cover and refrigerate for 1–2 hours.

When you are ready to cook, fire up the barbecue ready for direct cooking (see page 9).

Thread the beef strips onto the skewers. Put the skewers on the grill directly above the fire, lower the lid and cook for 7–8 minutes, turning a few times until cooked to your liking.

To serve, pile the noodles onto plates and top with a beef skewer. Squeeze over the lime juice and scatter over the spring onions (scallions), coriander (cilantro) and chillies.

Serves 4
–
Direct
Cooking

RIBEYE STEAKS, BLUE CHEESE & CHIVE BUTTER

It is easier to cook a thick steak than a thin steak – thin ones tends to overcook on the inside as the outside caramelizes, while thick ones stay succulent. Slice the steaks for sharing.

2 × 4cm (1½in) thick ribeye steaks, 350–400g (10½–14oz) each
a drizzle of olive oil
sea salt and freshly ground black pepper

For the blue cheese and chive butter
100g (7 tbsp) butter, softened
100g (3½oz) Stilton (or other creamy blue cheese), chopped
a small bunch of chives, snipped

To serve
rocket (arugula) leaves
6–8 vine tomatoes, cut into thick slices
a drizzle of balsamic vinegar

To make the blue cheese and chive butter, mash the butter, cheese and chives in a small bowl using a fork. Season with black pepper. Scoop onto a sheet of baking parchment, roll up into a log and twist the ends of the paper in opposite directions to form a neat cylinder. Chill in the fridge.

When you are ready to cook, light the barbecue and set up the fire for direct cooking (see page 9). High heat is essential for searing steak, so give the grill time to heat up thoroughly.

Drizzle the steaks with olive oil and season generously with salt. Lay the steaks on the grill bars directly over the fire and cook for 5–6 minutes, flipping every 30 seconds, or until nicely caramelized. If the steaks have a strip of fat on the outside edges, use tongs to hold them vertically on their side to allow some of the fat to render off.

Using a digital probe thermometer (see page 8) is the best way to eliminate guesswork. Insert the thermometer into the thickest part of the steak, ensuring the tip is in the centre; if you go too far the probe will be too close to the grill bars on the other side and give an inaccurate reading.

The internal temperature should read 52°C (125°F) for rare, 60°C (140°F) for medium and 71°C (160°F) for well done. Remove from the grill when it's 5–8°C (9–14°F) below your preferred serving temperature. The temperature will continue to rise as it rests.

Resting is the most important step in cooking steak. A 10-minute rest will allow the fibres to relax and the meat temperature to even out. Simply transfer the steaks to a plate, cover with a sheet of baking parchment and top with a clean dish towel.

To serve, scatter the rocket (arugula) over a large platter, adding the tomato slices and a drizzle of balsamic vinegar. Slice the steaks into thick, juicy ribbons and pile on top of the salad. Top with slices of the blue cheese and chive butter, which will melt as you eat.

Serves 4
–
Direct Cooking

BURGERS WITH MUSHROOMS & HORSERADISH MAYO

Soy sauce and mushrooms pack an umami flavour bomb in this juicy, irresistible burger.

2 tbsp soy sauce
1 tbsp sesame oil
25g (1oz) fresh root ginger, grated
1 garlic clove, finely chopped
2 large portobello mushrooms
    (about 300g/10½oz)
800g (1lb 12oz) beef mince
    (ground beef)
2 tsp Marmite (optional)
sea salt and freshly ground
    black pepper

For the horseradish mayo
2–3 tbsp mayonnaise
2–3 tsp hot horseradish sauce,
    or to taste

To serve
4 burger buns
a large handful of rocket
    (arugula) leaves

In a small bowl, mix the soy sauce, sesame oil, ginger and garlic. Put the mushrooms, gill-side up, on a lipped plate and pour over the marinade. Set aside for 30 minutes–1 hour.

Put the mince (ground beef) in a mixing bowl, add the Marmite, if using, and season with salt and pepper. Use your hands to mix thoroughly then divide into 4 even-sized balls. Flatten each in your hands to form 1cm (½in) thick burgers. Set aside. You can make the burgers 1 day ahead and keep covered in the fridge.

In separate small bowl, mix the mayonnaise and horseradish and season with salt and pepper to taste.

When you are ready to cook, fire up the barbecue ready for direct and indirect cooking (see page 9).

Once the barbecue is hot, slide the mushrooms gill-side up onto the grill bars directly above the fire and cook for 10–15 minutes, or until they have softened and coloured on the undersides. Slide them off the direct heat to make space for the burgers, keeping them gill-side up.

Put the burgers on the barbecue directly over the fire. Use tongs to lift the mushrooms and pour any marinating liquid over the burgers to give an extra hit of flavour as they cook. Rest the mushrooms back off the heat, gill-side down this time, to finish cooking. Lower the lid. After 3–4 minutes, flip the burgers over and cook the other side for another 3–4 minutes with the lid lowered.

When the burgers are cooked through, the internal temperature should read 71°C (160°F), slide them off the heat. Toast the buns directly over the fire for 1–2 minutes.

To build your burger, put a few rocket (arugula) leaves on the bun base and top with a burger. Cut the mushrooms into thick juicy slices and divide between the burgers. Finish with a good dollop of mayonnaise and top with the burger bun lid. Serve immediately.

Makes 4
–
Direct +
Indirect
Cooking

'FATTY' WITH BACON, CHEESE & TOMATO RELISH

A 'fatty' is a barbecued meatloaf wrapped in a savoury woven blanket of bacon and stuffed with cheese. What's not to like?

16 slices smoked streaky bacon
400g (14oz) beef mince (ground beef)
2 tbsp barbecue spice rub
100g (3½oz) mature Cheddar, grated
3 tbsp spicy tomato relish
sea salt and freshly ground
    black pepper

Fire up the barbecue ready for indirect cooking so you can cook the fatty away from the high heat of the fire (see page 9). Add a chunk of smoking wood to the fire for extra smokiness (see page 7).

Begin by making the woven bacon blanket to enclose the fatty. Vertically line up 8 of the bacon slices next to each other on a flat baking sheet. Working left to right, fold every other slice in half upwards. Lay a slice horizontally across the centre of the vertical slices. Unfold the vertical slices back over the horizontal one then fold up the other set of vertical slices. Lay over another horizontal slice and unfold the folded ones. Repeat to form a neat interwoven blanket.

Arrange the beef mince (ground beef) over the bacon in an even layer. Sprinkle over the barbecue rub and season with salt and pepper. Sprinkle the cheese in a line down the centre, then dollop over the relish.

Roll up the fatty as tightly as you can into a neat, fat, sausage shape. Take the fatty to the grill and rest on the grill bars, seam side down, away from the fire. Lower the lid and cook gently for 35–40 minutes, using tongs to turn it a few times so it browns evenly. Use a digital probe thermometer to check the internal temperature. It is cooked when it reads 65–70°C (150–160°F).

Let the fatty rest for a few minutes before carving into thick slices. You can stuff into buns and eat like a burger, or have it on its own like a meatloaf.

Serves 4–6
–
Indirect Cooking

Beef

PHILLY CHEESESTEAK

A truly indulgent treat. If Brie isn't your thing, feel free to swap it for a different cheese. Stilton or a similar creamy blue would be an excellent choice.

1 tbsp olive oil, plus extra to drizzle
25g (1¾ tbsp) butter
1 large onion, sliced
1 tsp smoked paprika
200g (7oz) chestnut mushrooms, sliced
a small handful of flat-leaf parsley, chopped
250g (9oz) steak (I use thin minute steaks)
150g (5½oz) Brie
4 slices sourdough bread
sea salt and freshly ground black pepper

Fire up the barbecue ready for direct and indirect cooking (see page 9).

Use a small fireproof (no wooden or plastic handles) frying pan (skillet). Drizzle in the olive oil and add the butter. Set onto the grill bars away from the fire and allow the butter to melt. Add the onions, smoked paprika and a good seasoning of salt and pepper. Lower the lid and cook gently for 15 minutes, or until the onion starts to caramelize, stirring now and then. Add the mushrooms and parsley and continue to cook gently until the onions are deep golden and the mushrooms tender.

Drizzle a little oil onto the steak and season with salt. Lay the steak on the grill bars directly over the fire and cook for 1–2 minutes on each side. You want to get a good exterior sear without overcooking the centre so a high heat is important. If necessary, add a little more fuel to the fire and, if you can, set your grill bars low near the coals.

Remove the steak and let it rest for 1–2 minutes while you assemble the sandwiches. Spread 2 slices of bread with the onion and mushroom mixture and top with the Brie. Slice the steak thinly across the grain and divide between the sandwiches. Top with the remaining slices of bread, pressing down gently.

Carefully slide each sandwich onto the grill bars directly over the fire and toast for 1–2 minutes. Use a metal spatula to flip over and toast the other side. Leave to rest for 1–2 minutes (the cheese will be very hot) then slice in half to serve.

Serves 2
–
Direct +
Indirect
Cooking

CHEDDAR, CORN & CHILLI 'SMASH' BURGERS

A 'smash' burger is just what it sounds like: you crush balls of burger mixture onto a hot surface, creating lots of irresistible, crunchy edges.

2 tbsp olive oil
2 shallots, thinly sliced
200g (7oz) can sweetcorn (corn), drained
a good pinch of chipotle (or other) chilli flakes
12 slices smoked streaky bacon
600g (1lb 5oz) beef mince (ground beef)
250g (9oz) Cheddar, sliced
sea salt and freshly ground black pepper

To serve
4 brioche burger buns, sliced open
a handful of lettuce leaves

You will also need a chapa or heavy-duty baking sheet and a cloche or large metal bowl (see pages 8–9).

Fire up the barbecue ready for direct cooking (see page 9). Set a chapa (see page 8) onto the grill bars (or improvise using a heavy-duty baking sheet), directly over the fire so it gets really hot.

Once it is hot, pour in the oil, add the shallots, sweetcorn (corn) and chilli, tossing to mix. Lower the lid and cook, stirring 1 or 2 times, until the shallots and sweetcorn are lightly charred, about 10 minutes. Scoop into a bowl and set aside.

Add the bacon to the chapa and grill until crisp, then move off the direct heat and keep warm.

Divide the mince (ground beef) into 4 even-sized balls. One at a time, place the mince balls on the hot chapa and use a spatula to firmly press them down to form burgers 1cm (½in) thick. Season the burgers with salt and pepper and lower the lid.

After 1 minute, flip the burgers over, season the other side and top each with a spoonful of the sweetcorn and onion mixture followed by the cheese slices. Place the lids of the buns on top of the burgers. Have the cloche (or large metal bowl) at the ready then sprinkle 2 tbsp water onto the chapa around the burgers and quickly cover with the cloche. Cook for 2 minutes. The steam will help to melt the cheese and soften the buns.

To serve, place a few lettuce leaves on the base of each bun, followed by 3 bacon slices. Use a spatula to slide the burgers, complete with lids, onto the burger bases, scraping up any loose crispy bits of cheese and sweetcorn and tucking them into the bun. Eat straightaway while piping hot.

Makes 4
–
Direct Cooking

SUYA BEEF & AUBERGINE SKEWERS

Suya are intensely spicy peanut-crusted beef skewers from Nigeria. You could tone down the heat by reducing the chilli powder a little, if you prefer.

500g (1lb 2oz) lean beef steak,
  sliced into 2cm (¾in) chunks
2 aubergines (eggplants), quartered
  and cut into 1cm (½in) wedges
2 tbsp vegetable oil
75g (2½oz) salted peanuts
1 tbsp chilli powder
1 tbsp garlic powder
2 tsp smoked paprika
1 tsp ground ginger
½ nutmeg, freshly grated
1 tsp salt

You will also need 8 metal skewers.

Put the steak and aubergine (eggplant) chunks in a shallow dish, drizzle over the oil and toss well to coat.

Set a dry frying pan (skillet) over a medium heat on the hob (stovetop) and tip in the peanuts. Toast to a deep golden colour, about 3 minutes, then transfer to a spice mill or pestle and mortar.

Pulse briefly or grind to a coarse powder. Tip into a bowl and stir in the chilli powder, garlic powder, paprika, ginger, nutmeg and salt. Sprinkle the spicy peanut powder over the beef and aubergine chunks and toss to thoroughly coat.

Thread the beef and aubergine onto the skewers, sprinkle over any leftover peanut and spice rub and press it into the surface. Cover and chill in the fridge for 2 hours, longer if you have time.

When you are ready to cook, fire up your barbecue ready for direct cooking (see page 9).

Lay the skewers on the grill bars directly over the fire, lower the lid and cook for about 8 minutes, turning regularly until the meat is deeply coloured and cooked through and the aubergine is soft. Serve straightaway.

Makes 8
–
Direct
Cooking

SPICY ROAST BEEF WITH HONEY-GRILLED CARROTS

Roasting a large piece of beef takes time, patience and gentle cooking. A digital probe thermometer is useful for making sure the meat is cooked just the way you like it.

2 tbsp English (spicy yellow) mustard, plus extra to serve
1 tbsp soft brown sugar
2 tsp smoked paprika
1 tsp sea salt flakes
1 tsp freshly ground black pepper
1.5kg (3lb 5oz) beef silverside (bottom round) roast
600g (1lb 5oz) small carrots, scrubbed
1 tbsp olive oil
1 tbsp runny honey

Fire up the barbecue ready for direct and indirect cooking (see page 9).

In a small bowl, mix together the mustard, sugar, paprika, sea salt and pepper. Spread all over the beef, working it into any crevices, wearing rubber (household) gloves if your skin is sensitive to spices. If you want to get ahead, you can apply the spice rub to the beef, then cover it and leave in the fridge for 1–2 hours.

Once you are ready to cook, rest the beef on the grill bars as far away from the fire as you can and shut the lid. Leave to cook gently for 1–1½ hours until a digital probe thermometer inserted in the centre reads 50°C (120°F).

While the beef is cooking, plunge the carrots into a large pan of lightly salted boiling water and simmer for 5 minutes. Drain well and drizzle over the olive oil and honey, seasoning with a little salt and pepper.

When the beef has reached the correct temperature, move it directly over the fire to sear the outside. Open the lid to turn it regularly for 20 minutes, or until it is caramelized all over. Transfer to a plate to rest, loosely covered with baking parchment and a couple of clean dish towels.

While the beef is resting tip the carrots on the grill bars and cook directly over the flames for 10 minutes, turning regularly, until they are lightly charred all over. Slice and serve with extra mustard on the side.

Serves 4
–
Direct + Indirect Cooking

SIRLOIN STEAKS & CHIMICHURRI

Chimichurri is a punchy, fresh herb sauce from Argentina that's a perfect match for steak.

4 × 2–3cm (¾in–1¼in) thick
   sirloin steaks
1 tbsp olive oil
sea salt and freshly ground
   black pepper

For the chimichurri
a large bunch of flat-leaf parsley,
   finely chopped
1 tsp dried oregano
3 garlic cloves, finely chopped
1–2 red chillies, finely chopped,
   to taste
2 tbsp red wine vinegar
1 tsp caster (superfine) sugar
100ml (3½fl oz/7 tbsp) extra
   virgin olive oil

Fire up your barbecue ready for direct cooking (see page 9). High heat is essential for searing steak, so give the grill time to heat thoroughly.

To make the chimichurri, put the parsley, oregano, garlic, chillies, red wine vinegar and caster (superfine) sugar in a bowl and season with salt and pepper. Gradually pour in the extra virgin olive oil, whisking to form a sauce the consistency of a loose pesto. Set aside at room temperature for the flavours to mingle.

When the barbecue is hot, drizzle the olive oil over the steaks and season well with salt. Lay the steaks directly over the fire and sear on both sides until nicely caramelized. Keep flipping the steaks over every 30 seconds or so to get the best caramelized crust.

Using a digital probe thermometer (see page 8) is the best way to eliminate guesswork when cooking steak. Insert the thermometer into the thickest part of the steak, ensuring the tip is in the centre (if you go too far the probe will be too close to the grill bars on the other side and give an inaccurate reading).

The internal temperature should read 52°C (125°F) for rare, 60°C (140°F) for medium and 71°C (160°F) for well done. Remove from the grill when it's 5–8°C (9–14°F) below serving temperature. The temperature will continue to rise by as it rests.

Resting is the most important step in cooking steak. A 10-minute rest will allow the fibres to relax and the meat temperature to even out. Simply transfer the steaks to a plate, cover with a sheet of baking parchment and top with a clean dish towel.

Serve the steaks cut into thick slices with the chimichurri sauce alongside.

Serves 4
–
Direct
Cooking

Beef

LOADED STEAK NACHOS

A fantastic sharing dish; just be sure not to stint on the cheese for maximum ooze.

3 tbsp olive oil
2 garlic cloves, finely chopped
2 tsp cumin seeds
400g (14oz) can black beans,
    drained and rinsed
4 spring onions (scallions), chopped
a small bunch of coriander (cilantro),
    chopped
200g (7oz) salted tortilla chips
250g (9oz) grated cheese (use
    Monterey Jack, if you can find it, or
    a mix of Cheddar and mozzarella)
2–4 tbsp pickled jalapeños, to taste
400g (14oz) steak (I use feather steak
    but skirt (flank), bavette or minute
    steaks are all good)
1–2 tsp chipotle chilli flakes, to taste
sea salt and freshly ground
    black pepper

To serve
guacamole
sour cream

Fire up the barbecue ready for direct and indirect cooking (see page 9).

Pour 1½ tbsp of the olive oil into a large fireproof (no plastic or wooden handles) frying pan (skillet). Add the garlic and cumin seeds and set it directly over the fire, stirring and frying for 2–3 minutes, then add the beans. Cook for 5–10 minutes, mashing the beans gently with the back of a wooden spoon. Transfer the beans to a bowl and stir in the spring onions (scallions) and most of the coriander (cilantro), seasoning with salt and pepper.

Add one third of the tortilla chips to the pan, followed by a few spoonfuls of the bean mixture, a handful of cheese and one third of the jalapeños. Repeat with the rest of the tortilla chips, beans, cheese and jalapeños, building up another 2 layers. Set the pan onto the grill bars, away from the fire, for around 10 minutes with the lid lowered, so the cheese gently melts.

Drizzle the remaining oil over both sides of the steaks and season with a good sprinkle of salt and the chipotle flakes. Cook the steaks directly over the fire, searing them hot and fast, for 1–2 minutes on each side. Transfer to a plate, cover loosely with foil and leave to rest for 5 minutes.

Slice the steaks and pile on top of the nachos in the pan. If the cheese needs more melting, slide the pan over the direct heat for a final 2–3 minutes and lower the lid.

Scatter over the remaining coriander and serve with guacamole and sour cream on the side.

Serves 2–4
–
Direct
+ Indirect
Cooking

LAMB

Lamb's rich succulence works so
well with a little fire and smoke. It
can be fatty, so always set up your
grill for both direct and indirect
grilling (even if the recipe calls for
direct grilling). That way you can
move the meat away from the heat
to prevent flare-ups if need be.

BUTTERFLIED, SPICED LAMB LEG

Some simple butchery is needed to butterfly the lamb leg to remove the bone and flatten the meat out to a more regular thickness so it cooks evenly. It's a straightforward process, and it really doesn't matter if it looks a little rough around the edges.

1 leg of lamb, about 2kg (4lb 8oz)
2 tbsp cumin seeds
2 tbsp coriander seeds
2 tsp smoked paprika
3 garlic cloves, finely chopped
2 tbsp olive oil
2 tbsp sherry vinegar
zest and juice of 2 oranges
50g (1¾oz) dried cranberries, chopped
50g (1¾oz) shelled pistachios, toasted and chopped
a small bunch of flat-leaf parsley, chopped
sea salt and freshly ground black pepper

Lay the lamb leg fleshy side down on a chopping board. Starting at the thick end, use a sharp knife to cut through the meat down to the bone. Continue to make small slices on both sides, following the line of the bone as closely as possible and easing the meat away. Remove and discard the bone. Where the meat is thickest, make a few deep slashes to open the meat out further to a more even thickness. Set aside in a large shallow bowl while you make the marinade.

Set a small frying pan (skillet) over a medium heat on the hob (stovetop) then toast the cumin and coriander seeds for 1 minute. Tip into a pestle and mortar and roughly grind. Add the smoked paprika, garlic, olive oil, sherry vinegar and the zest and juice of 1 orange (reserve the other to serve). Season with salt and pepper, stir well, then pour the marinade over the lamb and rub it in all over, working it into the meat. Cover and leave to marinate for 2 hours at room temperature, or overnight in the fridge for maximum flavour.

Light the barbecue and set up the fire for indirect cooking (see page 9).

Rest the lamb on the grill bars away from the fire and shut the lid. Cook for 45 minutes, turning 2 or 3 times and basting with any leftover marinade. Use a digital probe thermometer (see page 8) to test the temperature of the lamb at the thickest point. For medium-rare, remove from the grill when the temperature is at 50°C (120°F). If you prefer it cooked less or more, adjust the temperature by 5 degrees or so. Rest on a plate covered loosely with foil for 10 minutes. The lamb will continue to cook a little as it rests and the temperature will continue to rise by about 5 degrees.

While the lamb is cooking, stir together the cranberries, pistachios, parsley and the zest of the reserved orange in a small bowl and season with salt and pepper. Serve the lamb on a platter, with the juice of the orange squeezed over, then scatter over the cranberry mixture before carving.

Serves 6–8
–
Indirect Cooking

SPICED LAMB KOFTE WITH SAFFRON & TAHINI DRESSING

Chilling the kofte is an important first step as it helps keep the meat securely wrapped to the skewers as it cooks.

500g (1lb 2oz) lamb mince (ground lamb)
1 small onion, grated
a small bunch of flat-leaf parsley, chopped
1 tbsp cumin seeds
1 tsp ground cinnamon
1 tsp chilli flakes
olive oil for drizzling
sea salt and freshly ground black pepper

For the dressing
a pinch of saffron
150ml (scant ⅔ cup) tahini
2 tbsp runny honey

For the quick-pickled onions
1 red onion, thinly sliced
1 tbsp caster (superfine) sugar
1 tsp sea salt flakes
2 tbsp red wine vinegar

To serve
a handful of baby salad leaves
4 flatbreads
a handful of chopped coriander (cilantro), chopped
chopped chilli, to taste

You will also need 4 metal skewers.

Put the lamb mince (ground lamb) in a mixing bowl and add the onion and parsley. Heat a small frying pan (skillet) over a medium heat on the hob (stovetop), add the cumin seeds, toast lightly, then roughly grind in a pestle and mortar. Add the ground cumin, cinnamon, chilli flakes and a grind of salt and pepper to the bowl with the lamb and mix well. Lightly knead the mixture to a smooth paste – to help it stick to the skewers.

Divide the mixture into 4 even-sized balls. Thread a skewer through the centre of each and shape into kofte, pressing firmly to secure. Chill in the fridge for 1 hour to firm up.

To make the dressing, put the saffron in a heatproof jug and pour over 100ml (7 tbsp) boiling water. Set aside for 10 minutes. Add the tahini and honey, season with salt and pepper then whisk until smooth. Chill until needed.

For the quick-pickled onions, put the red onion in a bowl, then use your hands to lightly massage with the sugar and sea salt to soften. Add the vinegar, mix well then set aside for 30 minutes.

When you are ready to cook, fire up the barbecue ready for direct cooking (see page 9).

Drizzle the kofte with olive oil, lay them onto the grill bars directly over the fire, lower the lid and cook for 15–20 minutes, turning regularly. If they are cooking too quickly, slide them away from the heat to cook more gently.

To serve, scatter a few salad leaves over each flatbread and top with a kofte. Drizzle over the dressing (serve the rest on the side) and add some quick-pickled onions. Scatter over the coriander (cilantro) and chilli before rolling up and tucking in.

Serves 4
–
Direct Cooking

SPICED LAMB STEAKS WITH APRICOT RELISH

If you can't get fresh apricots, canned apricots in natural juice are an excellent substitute.

1 tbsp cumin seeds
1 tbsp coriander seeds
1 tsp smoked paprika
1–2 tsp dried chilli flakes, to taste
1 tsp ground cinnamon
1 tsp ground ginger
2 tsp soft light brown sugar
2 garlic cloves, finely chopped
zest and juice of 1 lemon
2 tbsp olive oil, plus extra to drizzle
4 × 175g (6oz) lamb leg steaks
sea salt and freshly ground
    black pepper
steamed couscous, to serve

For the apricot salsa
4 fresh apricots, sliced in half
    (or use canned apricot halves
    in natural juice)
½ small red onion, grated
a small bunch of coriander (cilantro),
    chopped, plus extra to serve

Heat a small frying pan (skillet) over a medium heat on the hob (stovetop). Toast the cumin and coriander seeds for 1–2 minutes until fragrant then grind coarsely in a pestle and mortar. Add the smoked paprika, chilli flakes, cinnamon, ginger, brown sugar, garlic, lemon zest and juice and a good grind of black pepper. Stir in the olive oil to make a paste.

Lay the lamb steaks on a large plate and rub all over with the spice paste. Cover and marinate in the fridge for 2 hours.

When you are ready to cook, fire up the barbecue ready for direct cooking (see page 9).

For the salsa, drizzle a little oil over the apricot halves and grill directly over the fire for 3–4 minutes, or until lightly charred and softened, turning halfway. Remove from the barbecue and chop, scooping into a bowl as you go. Stir in the onion, coriander (cilantro) and a little more olive oil. Season with salt and pepper and set aside while you cook the lamb.

Lay the lamb onto the grill bars directly over the fire, lower the lid and cook for 3–4 minutes on each side. A digital probe thermometer (see page 8) will read 55°C (130°F) for medium-rare. Cook for a few minutes more or less, depending on your preference.

To serve, pile the couscous onto a serving plate, slice the lamb on top and spoon the relish on the side. Sprinkle with a little extra coriander.

Serves 4
–
Direct
Cooking

Lamb

SMOKED BALSAMIC LAMB SHANKS WITH GREMOLATA

It is really worth getting the best, sweetest balsamic you can get your hands on for this recipe.

4 × 500g (1lb 2oz) lamb shanks
1 tbsp olive oil
4 tbsp balsamic vinegar
sea salt and freshly ground black
    pepper

For the gremolata
zest of 2 lemons
a generous handful of flat-leaf parsley,
    finely chopped
2 garlic cloves, finely chopped

You will also need 4 sheets of foil to wrap the shanks.

Fire up the barbecue ready for indirect cooking so you can cook the shanks away from the high heat of the fire (see page 9). Add a chunk of smoking wood to the fire for extra smokiness (see page 7).

Drizzle the lamb shanks with olive oil and rub in well all over. Season generously with salt and freshly ground black pepper. Rest the shanks onto the grill bars as far away from the fire as you can and shut the lid. Cook gently for 1½ hours, turning every 30 minutes, or until the meat is starting to come away from the bone.

Remove the shanks from the barbecue and shut the lid to preserve the heat.

Rest each shank in the centre of a sheet of foil and drizzle over the balsamic vinegar, tossing the shanks so they get a good coating. Seal the foil up tight to make parcels. Return to the grill, again, away from the fire, lower the lid and cook for a further 30 minutes.

Meanwhile, to make the gremolata, combine the lemon zest, parsley and garlic in a small bowl. Season with salt and freshly ground black pepper.

To serve, partly unwrap each parcel to reveal the shanks and rest on warmed plates. Sprinkle over the gremolata just before tucking in.

Serves 4
–
Indirect Cooking

LEMONY LAMB AND FETA MEATBALLS

These punchy meatballs can be prone to sticking so make sure you give your grill bars a really good scrub with a wire brush once the fire is hot.

500g (1lb 2oz) lamb mince
    (ground lamb)
zest of 1 lemon
2 garlic cloves, finely chopped
1 tbsp fresh oregano, chopped
    or 1 tsp dried oregano
200g (7oz) feta, crumbled
3 tbsp olive oil
1 red onion, finely chopped
a pinch of chilli flakes (optional)
500ml (generous 2 cups)
    tomato passata
1–2 tsp sugar
2 spring onions (scallions), chopped
sea salt and freshly ground black
    pepper
crusty bread, to serve

Fire up the barbecue ready for direct and indirect cooking (see page 9).

Put the lamb mince (ground lamb) in a mixing bowl, add the lemon zest, garlic, oregano, most of the feta (reserve some to serve) and a grind of salt and pepper. Roll the mixture into walnut-sized balls, setting aside on a plate as you go.

Set a fireproof pan (no plastic or wooden handles) on the grill bars, away from the fire to cook indirectly, and pour in the olive oil. Add the onion and chilli, if using, season with salt and pepper, lower the lid and cook gently for 10–15 minutes, stirring 1 or 2 times, until the onion is lightly caramelized and soft. Add the passata, stir in the sugar, lower the lid and cook gently for a further 20 minutes, stirring 1 or 2 times.

At the same time as you add the passata, lay the meatballs directly on the grill bars directly over the fire and leave to grill for about 20 minutes, turning a few times until crisp and golden. They may stick at first. Test one by teasing up an edge with a metal spatula – if it feels stuck leave for another 2 minutes before trying again. They will stick less after you have turned them once.

Once the meatballs are all cooked, drop them into the sauce. Scatter over the reserved feta and the spring onions (scallions), then slide the tin over the direct heat and lower the lid for a final 5 minutes.

Serve straight from the pan with plenty of bread to mop up the sauce.

Serves 4

–

Direct +
Indirect
Cooking

SPICY COCONUT LAMB CHOPS

The mint adds a welcome hit of freshness to these richly spiced chops so be generous!

8 cardamom pods
250ml (generous 1 cup)
   coconut cream
2 garlic cloves, finely chopped
50g (1¾oz) fresh root ginger,
   grated
1 tsp ground turmeric
a small bunch of coriander
   (cilantro), chopped
8 × 75–85g (2½oz–3oz)
   lamb chops, 600–700g
   (1lb 5oz–1lb 9oz), in total
25g (1oz) cashews
sea salt and freshly ground
   black pepper
a handful of mint, chopped,
   to garnish

Bruise the cardamom pods in a pestle and mortar until they open. Remove and discard the papery shells then grind the seeds to a coarse powder. Transfer to a shallow bowl and mix with the coconut cream, garlic, ginger, turmeric and coriander (cilantro). Add the lamb chops and coat them thoroughly with the coconut mixture. Cover and leave to marinate in the fridge for at least 2 hours, longer if you have time.

When you are ready to cook, fire up the grill ready for direct cooking (see page 9).

When the grill is hot, tip the cashews into a small fireproof pan (no plastic or wooden handles) and set over the fire. Toast for 1–2 minutes then chop roughly. Set aside. You can also do this on the hob (stovetop) inside if you want to get ahead.

Lay the chops directly over the fire, lower the lid and grill for 3 minutes on each side until lightly charred. Remove and leave to rest on a plate for 5 minutes before serving. If the fat from the chops is causing the fire to flare up as they cook, move them slightly away from the heat source.

To serve, pile the chops onto a platter and sprinkle over the cashews and mint.

Serves 4
–
Direct
Cooking

Lamb

HARISSA LAMB, PEPPER & DATE KEBABS

The dates are a little unusual here but they add a lovely hit of sweet stickiness. Make sure you get nice soft dates, which will grill best.

500g (1lb 2oz) lamb neck fillet, cut into 1cm (½in) pieces
2 red peppers, cut into 2cm (¾in) pieces
2 tbsp harissa
200g (7oz) soft dates, cut in half, stones removed
1 tbsp olive oil
sea salt and freshly ground black pepper

To serve
1 lemon, halved
a handful of chopped mint, to garnish

You will also need 6 metal skewers.

Put the lamb and pepper pieces in a bowl, add the harissa and a grind of salt and pepper and mix together. Cover and marinate in the fridge for 1–2 hours, longer if you have time.

When you are ready to cook, fire up the barbecue ready for direct cooking (see page 9).

Thread the lamb, peppers and dates alternately onto the skewers and drizzle over the olive oil.

Lay the skewers on the grill bars directly over the fire and cook for 2–3 minutes on each side until the lamb is cooked and the peppers lightly charred.

Squeeze over the lemon juice and sprinkle on the mint just before serving.

Serves 6
–
Direct Cooking

FISH & SEAFOOD

Seafood is brilliant to barbecue, although it has a reputation for being tricky. The key to prevent sticking is to cook hot and fast, and to only cook on clean grill bars. A fish cage is an excellent bit of kit that will help you to turn delicate fish easily.

CAJUN FISH TACOS WITH SLAW & LIME CREAM P

These are best made with corn tortillas. They can be hard to find in supermarkets but you can easily buy them online. If you can't get them, use small wheat tortillas instead.

3 tbsp cornflour (cornstarch)
2 tsp cumin seeds, toasted and ground
1 tsp cayenne pepper (or other chilli powder)
4 × 175g (6oz) firm white fish fillets (e.g. hake, cod or haddock)

For the slaw
½ red cabbage, finely shredded
3 spring onions (scallions), thinly sliced
25g (1oz) coriander (cilantro), chopped
1 heaped tbsp soft brown sugar
zest and juice of 1 lime
sea salt and freshly ground black pepper

For the lime cream
4 tbsp sour cream
2 tbsp mayonnaise
1 garlic clove, finely chopped
zest and juice of 1 lime
2 tbsp olive oil, plus extra to drizzle

To serve
12 small soft corn tortillas
chilli sauce (optional)
2 ripe avocados, sliced

Begin with the slaw as its flavour will improve after 1 hour in the bowl. Stir together the cabbage, spring onions (scallions), most of the coriander (cilantro) (save some to garnish) and half the sugar. Add the zest and juice of 1 lime and season generously with salt and pepper. Set aside at room temperature.

Sprinkle the cornflour (cornstarch) onto a large plate and stir in the cumin, cayenne and the remaining sugar. Season well with salt and pepper. Cut the fish fillets into chunky strips 3–4cm (1¼–1½in) wide. Toss the fish pieces in the seasoned flour to coat.

It's best to cook fish in a fish cage (see page 8) for easy turning and to minimize sticking. Lay the fish pieces snugly together on the fish cage ready for the grill. Fire up the barbecue ready for direct grilling (see page 9). For cooking fish it's good to have a really hot, clean grill surface so give the bars a good scrub with a wire brush when they're hot, even if you are using a fish cage.

While the grill is heating, make the lime cream. In a small bowl, stir together the sour cream, mayonnaise, garlic and the zest and juice of the lime. Season with salt and pepper.

Divide the tortillas into two piles of 6, wrap each in foil and set onto the grill bars to warm up for 2 minutes, turning them halfway. Set aside to keep warm while you cook the fish.

Generously drizzle olive oil over both sides of the fish and lay the cage onto the grill bars over the fire. Lower the lid and cook for 2–3 minutes on each side until lightly charred and cooked through.

To serve, spoon some slaw into the centre of each warmed tortilla and top with a few slices of avocado. Use forks to flake the fish and add a few large chunks to each tortilla. Drizzle with some of the lime cream and scatter over the remaining coriander. Add chilli sauce if you like. Fold up the sides and tuck in quick!

Serves 4
–
Direct Cooking

PORTUGUESE-STYLE TUNA STEAKS & STICKY ONIONS P

Port may seem like an unusual choice for fish, but the sweet stickiness really works with rich, meaty tuna steaks.

3 fresh bay leaves
2 garlic cloves, finely chopped
2 tbsp red wine vinegar
2 tbsp olive oil
4 × 150g (5½oz) fresh tuna steaks
sea salt and freshly ground black
    pepper

For the sticky onions
50g (4 tbsp) butter
1 tbsp olive oil
3 large onions, sliced
4 tbsp Port (port wine), of any type

To serve
cooked white rice
a handful of coriander (cilantro),
    chopped

For the sticky onions, heat the butter and oil in a frying pan (skillet) set over a medium-low heat on the hob (stovetop). Once the butter has melted, add the onions and allow to caramelize very gently for 40 minutes, stirring every now and then to cook evenly. Pour in the Port (port wine) and season well with salt and pepper. Turn up the heat and reduce the wine for a further 10 minutes.

While the onions are cooking, marinate the tuna. Use a sharp knife to remove the tough central ribs from the bay leaves then finely chop the leaves. Put the chopped bay leaves in a shallow dish large enough to hold the tuna steaks in a single snug layer. Add the garlic, vinegar and olive oil, stir to mix well, then add the tuna steaks, turning over in the marinade to coat. Cover and leave to marinate for 30 minutes.

Fire up the barbecue ready for direct grilling (see page 9). Once hot, give the grill bars a good scrub with a wire brush to help prevent the fish from sticking.

Lay the tuna steaks on the hot grill bars over the fire, lower the lid and cook for 2–3 minutes, turn carefully, then cook for a further 2–3 minutes.

To serve, spoon the rice onto plates and sprinkle over the coriander (cilantro). Add a tuna steak and a generous dollop of onions to each and serve the remaining onions on the side.

Serves 4
–
Direct
Cooking

MUSSELS WITH CHORIZO & GARLIC BUTTER

Surf and turf, Spanish-style! The bread here is essential to mop up all the rich, spicy juices.

1kg (2lb 4oz) mussels
50g (4 tbsp) butter
125g (4½oz) dried chorizo,
    diced into 1cm (⅛in) cubes
2 fat garlic cloves, sliced
1 heaped tsp smoked paprika
150ml (scant ⅔ cup) white wine
a handful of flat-leaf parsley, chopped
olive oil, to drizzle
1 ciabatta, sliced
sea salt and freshly ground
    black pepper

Put the mussels in a colander and rinse well under cold running water. Discard any broken mussels or any open mussels that don't shut when given a sharp tap against the edge of the colander. Pull away and discard any beard-like threads. Set aside.

Fire up the barbecue ready for direct grilling (see page 9).

Once the grill is hot, set a deep fireproof (no plastic or wooden handles) frying pan (skillet) over the fire. When hot, melt the butter in the pan, then add the chorizo and fry for 3–4 minutes, or until it is getting crisp around the edges.

Stir in the garlic and smoked paprika and season generously with salt and pepper. Cook, stirring, for 2–3 minutes then tip in the prepared mussels, pour in the wine and add the parsley, tossing everything together.

Cover the pan loosely with foil and shut the barbecue lid. Leave to steam for about 5 minutes. The cooking time will depend on how hot your fire is and how close the pan is to the embers. The mussels are ready when they have all opened up.

Slide the pan of mussels off the heat away from the fire to keep warm.

Drizzle a little olive oil over the sliced ciabatta and season both sides with salt and pepper. Rest on the grill bars directly over the fire to toast for 2–3 minutes, turning halfway.

To serve, rest the pan of mussels on a wooden board on the table and tuck straight in, using the toasted bread to mop up the juices. Discard any mussels that have not opened.

Serves 2
–
Direct Cooking

PANCETTA-WRAPPED HADDOCK & BUTTERY LEEKS

The wrapping of pancetta protects the fish from the fierce heat and makes the fillets less likely to stick. A fish cage is still useful as you can turn all the fillets over at once.

4 × 125–150g (4½–5½oz) chunky
    smoked haddock fillets
12 slices smoked pancetta
olive oil, for drizzling and brushing
4 slim leeks, about 3cm
    (1¼in) in diameter
75g (⅓ cup) butter
a few sprigs of thyme, plus
    extra picked leaves, to garnish
a splash of white wine
sea salt and freshly ground
    black pepper

A fish cage (see page 8) is useful.

Fire up the barbecue ready for direct and indirect cooking (see page 9).

Lay the haddock fillets on a chopping board and wrap 3 slices of pancetta snugly around each fillet to enclose. Drizzle with olive oil and season lightly with salt and pepper.

Slice the leeks lengthways almost to the root, leaving 4cm (1½in) intact so the leaves remain attached. Turn and cut through the other side so that the leek is cut into quarters lengthways, but attached at the root. Rinse well under cold running water and shake dry. Brush the leeks with olive oil from top to bottom and in between the leaves. Season with salt and pepper.

Lay the leeks over the grill bars, so they cook directly over the fire. Lower the lid and allow to lightly char for 10 minutes, turning regularly. Once the leeks have charred, slide them off the heat to keep warm. Put the butter and thyme sprigs in a fireproof tin or frying pan (no wooden or plastic handles) and set over the fire to melt. Add the leeks, pour in the wine, then slide the tin or frying pan away from the fire so the leeks finish cooking over a gentle indirect heat.

Give the grill bars a good scrub with a wire brush to clean them. Lay the wrapped haddock fillets onto the grill bars directly over the fire (in the fish cage, if using), lower the lid and cook for 10–12 minutes, turning a few times, until the pancetta is crisp and the fish is cooked. A probe thermometer (see page 8) is useful to check the fish. It will read 60°C (140°F) in the centre when it is cooked.

To serve, place a charred leek on each plate. Top with the cooked fish fillets, drizzle over the buttery leek juices and scatter over the thyme leaves.

Serves 4

–

**Direct +
Indirect
Cooking**

PRAWN, CHORIZO & CIABATTA SKEWERS

The spicy oil from the chorizo soaks into the bread so it grills up to be deliciously crisp and tasty. Keep the bread cubes fairly generous so they will be less likely to fall off the skewers.

6 thick slices ciabatta
2 tbsp olive oil
200g (7oz) raw peeled prawns (shrimp)
125g (4½oz) dried chorizo,
    cut into 5mm (¼in) discs
sea salt and freshly ground
    black pepper

To serve
a handful of flat-leaf parsley, chopped
1 lemon, quartered

You will also need 6 metal skewers.

When you are ready to cook, fire up your barbecue ready for direct cooking (see page 9).

Cut the bread into cubes a similar size to the diameter of the chorizo and put in a bowl. Drizzle in the olive oil. Add the prawns (shrimp) and the chorizo and a good grind of salt and pepper then toss to mix. Thread onto skewers, alternating between bread, prawns and chorizo.

Lay the skewers directly over the fire and cook them for 3–5 minutes, turning regularly, until the prawns are pink and cooked through and the bread is crisp. If the bread is catching too quickly, move the skewers slightly further away from the fire to cook more gently.

To serve, scatter over the parsley and squeeze over the lemon. Eat while hot.

Makes 6
–
Direct Cooking

SALMON, COURGETTE & LEMON KEBABS P

A fish cage is useful for cooking the kebabs. It will help prevent sticking and you can turn all the skewers in one go.

500–600g (1lb 2oz–1lb 5oz) chunky skinless salmon fillets
2 medium courgettes (zucchini)
1 lemon
2 tbsp olive oil
sea salt and freshly ground black pepper

For the herby yogurt sauce
250g (9oz) Greek yogurt
a handful of mixed fresh herbs (parsley, coriander/cilantro, chives), chopped
1 garlic clove, finely chopped

To serve
boiled new potatoes
green salad with sliced avocado

You will also need 4 metal skewers and, ideally, a fish cage (see page 8).

Fire up the barbecue ready for direct grilling (see page 9). Once hot give the grill bars a good scrub with a wire brush to clean them. Clean, hot grill bars minimize sticking, even if you are using a fish cage.

Cut the salmon fillets into 2–3cm (¾in–1¼in) cubes. Use a vegetable peeler to slice the courgettes (zucchini) into thin ribbons. Cut the lemon into quarters and then slice each quarter into 2–3mm (⅛in) slices.

Take a skewer and thread a piece of salmon onto it, then fold up a ribbon of courgette and thread that on, followed by a piece of lemon. Repeat until you have used all the skewers and remaining salmon, courgettes and lemon slices. Drizzle over the olive oil, season with salt and pepper and set aside. If you are using a fish cage, line up the kebabs in it.

For the sauce, mix the ingredients thoroughly in a bowl, seasoning with salt and pepper to taste.

Lay the kebabs (in a fish cage, if using) onto the grill bars directly over the fire and cook for a couple of minutes on each side, or until the fish is just cooked through. Using a metal spatula to help turn will help you ease off any areas that are a bit stuck.

Serve hot from the grill with the potatoes and salad and yogurt sauce alongside.

Serves 4
–
Direct Cooking

Fish & Seafood

GRILLED TROUT, CUCUMBER SALAD & BURNT LEMON P

Slicing deep cuts into each side of the fish increases the surface area and allows the heat to penetrate, so they cook more quickly.

4 × 250–300g (9–10½oz) fresh trout
a small handful of flat-leaf parsley
   stems
olive oil, for drizzling
2 lemons, halved
sea salt and freshly ground
   black pepper

For the cucumber salad
2 tbsp natural yogurt
2 tbsp mayonnaise
1–2 tsp red wine vinegar
25g (1oz) dill, chopped
zest of 1 lemon
1 cucumber, diced into 1cm
   (½in) cubes
½ red onion, thinly sliced
100g (3½oz) cherry tomatoes,
   halved

A fish cage (see page 8) is useful for turning the fish.

To make the cucumber salad, spoon the yogurt and mayonnaise into a mixing bowl. Add the vinegar, dill and lemon zest and season well with salt and pepper. Taste, adding more vinegar to sharpen if you like. Add the cucumber, onion and tomatoes and mix gently. Cover and chill until needed, up to 2 hours ahead.

Fire up the barbecue ready for direct grilling (see page 9).

Prepare the trout by slicing deep diagonal cuts through the skin on both sides. Stuff the parsley stems into the body cavity of each fish and drizzle a little oil over each one. Season on both sides with salt and pepper. Line up the fish in a fish cage, if you are using one. Make sure your grill bars are hot and clean them first using a wire brush to minimize sticking.

Grill the trout for about 6 minutes on each side, turning carefully, until cooked through and the skin is crisp. Rest the lemon halves on the grill at the same time, cut-side down, so the surface lightly burns and caramelizes.

Serve the fish with the cucumber salad alongside and the grilled lemons to squeeze over.

To serve a whole fish:

Lay it out flat on a plate and slice through the fish where the head meets the body, until the knife meets the backbone. Repeat at the tail end.

Slice through the fillet in the centre, separating the top fillet into two mini fillets, one either side of the backbone.

Then slide the knife underneath to ease the flesh of one mini fillet away from the bone, trying to keep it in one piece, if possible.

Repeat with the other mini fillet.

Lift the tail and pull up toward the head, easing the backbone away from the bottom fillet.

Serves 4
—
Direct Cooking

VEGETABLES

Vegetables come in a rainbow of colours and textures and
are brilliant to barbecue. Their flavour is elevated by
a little smoke and fire.

AUBERGINE WITH FETA, CURRANTS & PINE NUTS v

Aleppo pepper (also known as pul biber) is a type of chilli flake with a lovely lemony flavour. Find it online or in Turkish or Middle Eastern food shops.

3 medium aubergines (eggplants)
2 tbsp olive oil
75g (2½oz) pine nuts, toasted
75g (2½oz) currants
a handful of flat-leaf parsley, chopped
200g (7oz) feta, crumbled
extra virgin olive oil, for drizzling
1 lemon, halved
sea salt and freshly ground
    black pepper

To serve
seeds from 1 pomegranate
1 tsp Aleppo pepper flakes (optional),
    to garnish

Fire up the barbecue ready for indirect cooking so you can cook the aubergines (eggplants) away from the high heat of the fire (see page 9).

Slice the aubergines in half lengthways, then score a diamond pattern deeply into the cut surface of each half using a small sharp knife, taking care not to pierce the skin. Drizzle over the olive oil and season generously with salt and pepper.

Set the aubergine halves onto the grill bars, lower the lid and cook indirectly for 15 minutes, rotating once or twice so they cook evenly. You want them to soften all the way through, so keep them away from the direct fire. Turn and cook cut-side down for another 10 minutes with the lid down, until they are soft and tender. Cooking time will vary depending on the size of the aubergines.

Meanwhile, mix the pine nuts, currants and parsley in a bowl. Once the aubergines are tender, slide them, cut-side up, onto a fireproof baking sheet then scatter over the nut and herb mixture. Sprinkle over the feta and grind over some black pepper.

Slide the tray back onto the barbecue, this time over the direct heat, and leave to cook for a further 10–15 minutes, or until the cheese is softened.

Use a metal spatula to transfer the aubergines to a serving plate then drizzle with plenty of extra virgin olive oil and squeeze over the lemon juice. Scatter over the pomegranate seeds and a good sprinkle of Aleppo pepper, if you have some. Serve warm.

Serves 4–6
–
Indirect
Cooking

SQUASH, KALE & CANNELLINI BEAN SALAD v

Squash need gentle indirect heat to soften their dense flesh, so be sure to take your time to get them tender.

1 medium squash, about 1kg (2lb 4oz)
200g (7oz) cavolo nero (black kale)
400g (14oz) can cannellini beans,
   drained and rinsed
250g (1 cup) ricotta
50g (1¾oz) pumpkin seeds

For the dressing
4 tbsp olive oil, plus extra for brushing
a small bunch of coriander (cilantro),
   roughly chopped
1 garlic clove, roughly chopped
½ bunch of spring onions (scallions)
juice of 1 lime
2 tsp sugar
1 tsp hot sauce, or to taste
sea salt and freshly ground
   black pepper

Fire up the barbecue ready for direct and indirect cooking so you can cook the squash away from the high heat of the fire (see page 9).

Using a sharp knife, cut the squash in half. Scoop out and discard the seeds and membranes, then cut each half into quarters lengthways so you are left with 8 long thin wedges in total. Brush lightly with olive oil and season with salt and pepper. Lay the wedges onto the grill bars away from the fire to cook indirectly. Lower the lid and cook for 30 minutes, or until they are tender and lightly caramelized. Turn over and rotate the wedges a few times so they cook evenly.

Tear out and discard the thickest part of the stems from the cavolo nero. Brush the leaves with olive oil, season with salt, then set aside while the squash cooks.

For the dressing, put the olive oil, coriander (cilantro), garlic, spring onions (scallions), lime juice, sugar and hot sauce into a deep jug. Add 3 tbsp cold water and use a stick blender to pulse to a smooth sauce, adding a splash more water if necessary. Stir 2 tbsp of the dressing into the cannellini beans and set aside the rest of the dressing.

Once the squash is almost tender, lay the oiled cavolo nero leaves onto the grill bars directly over the fire, lower the lid and grill for 1–2 minutes on each side, or until the leaves are crisp.

To serve, spread the dressed beans over a serving plate. Top with the grilled squash wedges, add the ricotta in generous spoonfuls and sprinkle on the pumpkin seeds. Tear the crispy cavolo nero into pieces and scatter over the salad. Drizzle over the remaining dressing. Serve hot or at room temperature.

Serves 4–6
—
Direct +
Indirect
Cooking

Vegetables

CAULIFLOWER SATAY & PEANUT SAUCE VE

These spicy cauliflower kebabs are a little delicate but oh so worth it! Threading the florets through the stems will help them stay on the stick.

1 medium cauliflower,
   broken into florets

For the marinade
1 tbsp coriander seeds
1 tsp chilli flakes
1 tsp ground turmeric
1 banana shallot, finely chopped
⅓ × 400ml (14fl oz) can coconut milk
2 tbsp soy sauce
2 tsp soft brown sugar
2 garlic cloves, finely chopped

For the satay sauce
1 tbsp vegetable oil
2 banana shallots, finely chopped
2 garlic cloves, finely chopped
2.5cm (1 in) piece of fresh root
   ginger, grated
1 lemongrass stalk, finely chopped
⅔ × 400ml (14fl oz) can coconut milk
125g (4½oz) salted peanuts, roughly
   crushed
2 tbsp soy sauce
sea salt and freshly ground
   black pepper

To serve
steamed rice
chopped coriander (cilantro)
sliced spring onions (scallions)
red chillies, to taste

You will also need 4–6 metal skewers.

For the marinade, put the coriander seeds in a small frying pan (skillet) on the hob (stovetop) and toast over a medium heat for 2 minutes. Roughly grind in a pestle and mortar then transfer to a large bowl. Add the chilli flakes, turmeric, shallot, coconut milk (reserve the remainder of the can for later), soy sauce, brown sugar and garlic. Season with salt and pepper and stir well.

Bring a large pan of lightly salted water to the boil, then add the cauliflower florets. Blanch for 5 minutes until starting to soften. Drain well, add to the marinade then stir gently to coat the florets. Set aside to marinate for 2 hours.

To make the satay sauce, heat the oil in a small pan on the hob over a low heat. Add the shallots and gently soften for 15 minutes, stirring now and then, until golden. Add the garlic, ginger and lemongrass, fry for a further 5 minutes, then add the remainder of the can of coconut milk and the peanuts and soy sauce. Simmer for 5 minutes until thickened. Keep the sauce warm while you cook the cauliflower.

When you are ready to cook, fire up the barbecue ready for direct grilling (see page 9).

Thread the cauliflower florets carefully onto skewers, through the firm part of the stems. Take the leftover marinade to the barbecue and have a silicone pastry brush (see page 8) ready for basting. Lay the skewers on the grill bars, lower the lid and cook for 2–3 minutes, then baste and turn over. Keep cooking and basting for 10 minutes, or until the cauliflower is tender.

To serve, rest the skewers on a bed of rice and scatter over the coriander (cilantro), spring onions (scallions) and chillies. Serve the satay sauce alongside.

Serves 4–6
–
**Direct
Cooking**

AUBERGINE, STILTON & SUN-DRIED TOMATO ROLLS v

These make a wonderful nibble while you're cooking your main course. You could use firm crumbled goat's cheese instead of Stilton if you prefer.

2 large aubergines (eggplants)
2 tbsp olive oil
200g (7oz) Stilton or similar creamy
  blue cheese (vegetarian, if need be)
80g (2¾oz) sun-dried tomatoes,
  chopped
a few sprigs of fresh thyme,
  leaves picked
50g (1¾oz) walnuts, toasted
  and chopped
2 tbsp runny honey
sea salt and freshly ground
  black pepper

Fire up the barbecue ready for direct grilling (see page 9).

Cut the aubergines (eggplants) lengthways into 5mm (¼in) slices. Brush with olive oil and season with salt and pepper. Lay the aubergine slices onto the grill bars directly over the fire, lower the lid and cook for 12–15 minutes, turning a few times until lightly charred and soft.

To make the filling, gently stir together the Stilton, tomatoes, half of the thyme leaves (reserve the rest to garnish) and a good grind of black pepper. Keep it as a loose crumbly mixture, rather than mashing to a paste.

Transfer the aubergines to a baking sheet and divide the cheese mixture evenly between them. Roll up each slice and put seam-side down on the baking sheet. Once all the aubergines are rolled, rest the baking sheet on the grill bars and shut the barbecue lid. Cook for 5 minutes, or until the cheese starts to soften.

Transfer the rolls to a serving platter, scatter over the toasted walnuts and reserved thyme leaves and drizzle over the honey. Serve warm.

Serves 4
–
Direct
Cooking

Vegetables

PURPLE SPROUTING BROCCOLI & CAPER DRESSING

VE

A brilliantly easy side dish that's great with simple grilled salmon, or try the Salmon, Courgette & Lemon Kebabs on page 103.

300g (10½oz) purple sprouting broccoli
300g (10½oz) asparagus
1 tbsp olive oil
50g (1¾oz) blanched almonds
100ml (7 tbsp) extra
    virgin olive oil
40g (1½oz) capers, roughly chopped
2 garlic cloves, sliced
a small bunch of flat-leaf parsley,
    chopped
sea salt and freshly ground
    black pepper

Fire up your barbecue ready for direct grilling (see page 9).

If the purple sprouting broccoli has stems thicker than your little finger, first blanch it for 2 minutes in boiling water, then drain well and proceed as follows.

Spread out the purple sprouting broccoli and the asparagus on a baking sheet, drizzle over the 1 tbsp of olive oil and season with salt and pepper.

Toast the almonds in a small frying pan (skillet) on the hob (stovetop) set over medium heat for 2 minutes. Once they are golden in places, roughly chop and set aside in a small bowl.

Take a small fireproof pan (no wooden or plastic handles) and pour in the olive oil. Add the capers, garlic and parsley and season with salt and pepper.

Line up the purple sprouting broccoli and asparagus on the grill, laying it perpendicular to the grill bars so it doesn't fall through, and lower the lid. Cook for 8–10 minutes, turning a few times until lightly charred in places.

Set the pan with the olive oil dressing onto the grill bars away from the fire so it gently warms through as the vegetables cook.

Transfer the cooked broccoli and asparagus to a serving platter and pour over the warmed dressing. Scatter over the chopped almonds and serve while hot.

Serves 4–6
as a side
–
Direct
Cooking

SMOKED NEW POTATOES WITH OLIVE, CAPER & BASIL DRESSING VE

Think of this as a hot potato salad, a punchy side dish to all sorts of grilled dishes.

1kg (2lb 4oz) new potatoes, scrubbed and quartered
1 tbsp olive oil
1 red onion, finely chopped
3 garlic cloves, roughly chopped
200g (7oz) cherry vine tomatoes, vines snipped to make bunches of 3–4 tomatoes
sea salt and freshly ground black pepper

For the dressing
4 tbsp extra virgin olive oil
a large handful of fresh basil, finely shredded
3 tbsp pitted black olives, chopped
2 tbsp capers, chopped
1 tsp caster (superfine) sugar

Fire up the barbecue ready for direct and indirect cooking so you can cook the potatoes away from the high heat of the fire (see page 9). Add a chunk of smoking wood to the fire for extra smokiness (see page 7).

Put the potato quarters in a roasting tin, drizzle with the olive oil and season well with salt and pepper. Set the roasting tin on the grill away from the coals to cook indirectly. Shut the lid and cook for around 45 minutes, stirring a few times and rotating the tin so the potatoes cook evenly.

If the potatoes are softening but not getting crisp, slide the tin closer to the heat. Don't worry if the potatoes break up a bit. You want them to be soft and tender throughout with a few irresistible crispy edges here and there. Halfway through the cooking time, add the onion and garlic to the tin and stir through.

At the same time, put the tomatoes onto the grill bars, directly over the fire, and roast for 15 minutes, or until they are soft and lightly charred in parts but not collapsing. Use a metal spatula to turn them once halfway through the cooking time.

For the dressing, whisk the extra virgin olive oil, basil, olives, capers and sugar in a bowl. Season with plenty of pepper and set aside.

Remove the cooked potatoes from the grill and spoon over the dressing. Top with the grilled tomatoes and serve warm straight from the tin.

Serves 4–6 as a side
–
Direct + Indirect Cooking

PEACH, HALLOUMI & LENTIL SALAD v

Filling enough to be a main course, this colourful salad is a medley of textures and flavours and features that barbecue favourite, halloumi.

200g (7oz) puy lentils or similar
    small dark green lentils
1 small onion
2 garlic cloves, whole
2 bay leaves
2 tbsp balsamic vinegar,
    plus extra to drizzle
3 tbsp extra virgin olive oil,
    plus extra to drizzle
3 ripe peaches, quartered
2 × 225g (8oz) packs of halloumi, sliced
80g (2¾oz) watercress
sea salt and freshly ground
    black pepper

To serve
a small bunch of mint, chopped
2–3 red chillies, chopped

Put the lentils into a small saucepan and add cold water to cover. Quarter the onion through the root (no need to peel) and add to the pan with the garlic and bay leaves. Set on the hob (stovetop) over a medium heat and bring to the boil.

Simmer for 10–15 minutes until the lentils are tender but with a little bite. Drain and discard the onion, garlic and bay. While still hot, add the balsamic vinegar, olive oil and a grind of salt and pepper, stirring well to mix.

Fire up the barbecue ready for direct cooking (see page 9).

Drizzle the peaches and halloumi with olive oil and season with salt and pepper. Rest on the grill bars directly over the fire. Lower the lid and and grill for 2–3 minutes, then turn over to cook the other side. Transfer to a plate.

To serve, pile the watercress into a serving plate or bowl and toss through the dressed lentils. Top with the grilled peaches and halloumi and scatter over the mint and chilli.

Finish with a good drizzle of extra virgin olive oil and balsamic and serve warm.

Serves 4–6
–
Direct
Cooking

Vegetables

GRILLED RATATOUILLE & BLACK OLIVE TAPENADE P

The sunshine flavours of the Mediterranean on a plate!

2 Romano peppers
1 aubergine (eggplant)
1 courgette (zucchini)
8 plum tomatoes
3 tbsp olive oil
sea salt and freshly ground
    black pepper
a small handful of basil leaves,
    roughly chopped, to serve

For the tapenade
100g (3½oz) pitted black olives
1 tbsp capers
3 anchovy fillets (optional;
    omit if vegetarian)
2 garlic cloves
50ml (3 tbsp) extra virgin olive oil
1 tbsp red wine vinegar

Fire up the barbecue ready for direct grilling (see page 9).

To make the tapenade, whizz the olives, capers, anchovies, if using, garlic, olive oil and vinegar in a food processor until smooth. Season with pepper, but no salt (the olives are salty enough). Scoop into a bowl and set aside.

Slice the peppers into quarters lengthways and remove and discard the seeds. Cut the aubergine (eggplant) lengthways into 8 long thin wedges. Cut the courgette (zucchini) into quarters lengthways. Slice the tomatoes in half lengthways. Spread the vegetables out on a baking sheet and drizzle with the olive oil. Season well with salt and pepper.

Transfer the oiled vegetables directly onto the grill bars over the fire, lower the lid and cook until they are soft, tender and lightly charred. Use tongs to turn them frequently, moving them around so they cook evenly. When the different types of vegetable are cooked, slide them off the heat onto the far side of your grill.

Transfer all the cooked vegetables to a serving plate and spoon some of the tapenade over the top, serving the rest in a bowl alongside. Scatter over the basil just before serving.

Serves 4–6
as a side
–
Direct
Cooking

MUSHROOMS, MOZZARELLA, PESTO, CRUMBS v

Mushrooms are truly brilliant to grill, soaking up lots of lovely smoke flavours.

6 large portobello mushrooms
400g (14oz) can cannellini beans,
    drained and rinsed
1 ball mozzarella, cut into 6 slices
2 tbsp fresh breadcrumbs
sea salt and freshly ground
    black pepper

For the pesto
25g (1oz) pine nuts
30g (1oz) basil (leaves and stems),
    chopped
25g (1oz) Parmesan (or vegetarian
    grating cheese)
1 garlic clove, chopped
3 tbsp olive oil, plus extra for drizzling
1 tsp red wine vinegar, or to taste

Fire up the barbecue ready for direct cooking (see page 9).

Toast the pine nuts in a small frying pan (skillet) over a medium heat on the hob (stovetop). Transfer to a pestle and mortar and grind coarsely. Add most of the chopped basil (saving a sprinkle to garnish), the Parmesan and garlic and pound to a rough paste. Stir in the olive oil and vinegar and season to taste with salt and pepper.

Drizzle the mushrooms with olive oil then rest them on the grill bars directly over the fire, gill-side down. Shut the lid and cook for 10 minutes, or until softening. Transfer, gill-side up, to a fireproof roasting tin and use a small sharp knife to ease out the cooked stems. Chop the stems and scatter into the hollows of the mushrooms.

Spoon the beans equally into the hollows of the mushrooms. Top each mushroom with 1–2 teaspoons of pesto and a slice of mozzarella. Sprinkle over the breadcrumbs and finish with a drizzle of olive oil, then slide the tin back over the fire. Shut the lid and cook for a further 10–15 minutes until the cheese is melting and the breadcrumbs are crisping up.

Serve hot and bubbling from the grill, sprinkled with the remaining basil, with crusty bread to mop up the juices, if you like.

Serves 3–6
–
Direct
Cooking

Vegetables

PANEER & TOMATO SKEWERS v

Paneer is an Indian cheese that grills in a similar way to halloumi. It has a mild flavour and soaks up the spicy rub deliciously.

2 × 225g (8oz) blocks of paneer
2 tbsp garam masala
2 tbsp vegetable oil
200g (7oz) cherry tomatoes
sea salt and freshly ground black
    pepper
a handful of baby salad leaves, to serve

For the chutney
20g (¾oz) mint
20g (¾oz) coriander (cilantro)
1 garlic clove
juice of ½ lemon
1–2 green chillies, to taste
1 tsp sugar

You will also need 4 metal skewers.

Cut each block of paneer in half and rest on a plate.

Put the garam masala in a bowl, add the vegetable oil and salt and pepper to taste, then stir to a paste. Spoon a generous half of the paste over the paneer and rub all over. Cover and marinate in the fridge for 30 minutes–1 hour.

Add the cherry tomatoes to the bowl with the rest of the spiced oil and toss well to mix. Thread the tomatoes onto skewers.

To make the chutney, whizz the mint, coriander (cilantro), garlic, lemon juice, chillies and sugar in a mini blender until smooth, adding a splash of water if needed. Season to taste with salt and pepper.

When you are ready to cook, fire up the barbecue ready for direct grilling (see page 9).

Get the fire really hot and give the grill bars a clean with a wire brush to minimize sticking. Lay the paneer on the grill bars directly over the fire, lower the lid and cook for 2–3 minutes, or until a nice browned crust forms on the bottom. Using a metal spatula to ease the paneer away from the grill, flip over to cook the other side.

At the same time as you add the paneer, add the tomato skewers to the grill and cook until the tomatoes are lightly charred and starting to burst open.

Serve the paneer on a bed of salad leaves with the tomato skewers on top. Drizzle over some of the chutney and serve the rest alongside.

Serves 4
–
Direct Cooking

Vegetables

GRILLED CORN WITH 3 BUTTERS v

Grilled corn is a winner and adding one of these butters will elevate it to the next level. They freeze well so make extra and save some for another day.

4 large corn on the cob
(ideally in their husks)
100g (7 tbsp) butter, softened
sea salt and freshly ground black
pepper

For the garlic butter
1 garlic clove, crushed
2 tbsp chopped mixed fresh herbs
(such as chives, parsley, basil,
tarragon)

For the harissa butter
1 tbsp harissa
1 tbsp chopped coriander (cilantro)

For the Parmesan butter
10g (¼oz) freshly grated Parmesan
(or vegetarian grating cheese)
1 tbsp capers, chopped

If your corn is still in its husks, put them in a sink filled with cold water, soak for 30 minutes, then drain. Dampening the husks will create steam as they cook. If your corn is out of its husks, run each one briefly under the cold tap then wrap individually in 2 layers of foil.

Put the softened butter in a small bowl. Use a fork to mash through your chosen flavourings (for either garlic butter, harissa butter, or Parmesan butter) then season well with salt and pepper. Scoop onto a sheet of baking parchment and roll up into a neat log, twisting the ends in opposite directions to tighten the roll. Put in the freezer for 20–30 minutes to firm up.

Fire up the barbecue ready for direct grilling (see page 9).

Put the corn, either in its husks or in foil wrappers, directly over the fire, lower the lid and grill for 15–20 minutes, using tongs to turn from time to time. For the corn in their husks, the husks will be blackened and charred when it's ready. For the foil-wrapped corn, you will need to unwrap one to test if it's tender.

Serve the corn hot, with slices of the butter to melt over as you eat.

Serves 4
–
Direct
Cooking

SOMETHING SWEET

Finally, a few sweet treats to prove
that anything can be barbecued.
Don't be limited by this selection.
Let your imagination run wild
– figs, pears, nectarines or even
orange segments are all great
on the grill.

CINNAMON PLUMS & YOGURT PANCAKES v

Pancakes work brilliantly on the grill, although you do need to cook them on a flat surface. A chapa is perfect but you can also use a heavy-based frying pan if you don't have one.

300g (2½ cups)
    self raising (self rising) flour
300g (1¼ cups) Greek yogurt, plus
    extra to serve
150ml (scant ⅔ cup) milk
2 large eggs
1 tsp vanilla extract
4 tbsp caster (superfine) sugar
1 tsp ground cinnamon, plus extra
    to serve
400g (14oz) ripe plums, halved,
    stones (pits) removed
vegetable oil, for cooking the pancakes
maple syrup, to serve

You also need a chapa or plancha (see page 8) or a heavy-based frying pan (skillet).

Fire up the barbecue ready for direct and indirect cooking (see page 9). Once the grill is hot, give the bars a good scrub using a wire brush. Rest the chapa or plancha or heavy-duty frying pan (skillet) onto the grill bars directly over the fire. You need a really hot surface to cook pancakes so be patient!

While the grill is heating, make the pancake batter. Tip the flour into a large mixing bowl. Add the yogurt, milk, eggs, vanilla and 2 tbsp of the sugar and whisk to a thick smooth batter. Set aside.

On a small plate, mix the remaining 2 tbsp of sugar and the cinnamon. One by one, dip the plums cut-side down in the cinnamon sugar. Rest the plums cut-side up onto the grill bars away from the fire for a few minutes until they begin to soften. Once soft, turn the plums so they are sugar-side down and cook for a further 1 minute. Transfer to a plate and set aside.

When the chapa or plancha is hot, drizzle a little oil on a piece of scrunched-up paper towel and wipe across the surface. Drop dessertspoonfuls of batter onto the hot chapa, well spaced – they will spread as they cook.

Shut the lid and cook for 2–3 minutes. The pancakes are ready to turn when you see tiny bubbles appear on their surface. Use a metal spatula to flip them over and cook the other side. As they're cooked, remove them from the grill and repeat until you have used all the batter.

To serve, put a few pancakes on each plate and top with the grilled plums. Add a dollop of yogurt, a generous drizzle of maple syrup and a sprinkle of cinnamon before serving.

Makes 12–16
—
**Direct
+ Indirect
Cooking**

SPICED APPLE FRENCH TOAST & WHIPPED CREAM v

A brilliant brunch idea. If you don't have a chapa improvising with a frying pan or heavy-duty baking sheet is just fine.

For the French toast
2 eggs
2 tsp caster (superfine) sugar
½ tsp vanilla extract
150ml (scant ⅔ cup) milk
4 brioche rolls, sliced in half

For the spiced apples
3 eating (dessert) apples
juice of ½ lemon
2 tbsp demerara (light brown) sugar
1–2 tsp ground mixed spice
25g (1¾ tbsp) butter, plus a knob to cook the French toast

For the whipped cream
250ml (generous 1 cup) double (heavy) cream
2 tbsp icing (confectioners') sugar
1 tsp vanilla extract

You also need a chapa or plancha (see page 8) or a heavy-duty baking sheet.

Fire up the barbecue ready for direct and indirect cooking so you can cook the apple wedges away from the high heat of the fire (see page 9). Give the grill bars a good clean using a wire brush, then rest the chapa/plancha (or heavy-duty baking sheet) on the grill bars above the fire to heat up.

For the French toast, find a shallow dish large enough to fit the brioche in a single layer. Crack in the eggs, add the caster (superfine) sugar and vanilla and whisk lightly with a fork. Pour in the milk and whisk again. Lay the brioche roll halves in the dish, cut-side down, and set aside for 10 minutes, or until they have absorbed most of the liquid. Turn over and leave for a further 5 minutes.

Meanwhile, cut the apples into wedges and remove and discard the cores (no need to peel), dropping them onto a plate as you go. Squeeze over the lemon juice and toss to coat, then sprinkle over the demerara (light brown) sugar and ground mixed spice.

Pour the cream into a mixing bowl, add the icing (confectioners') sugar and vanilla. Whisk to soft peaks then cover and transfer to the fridge to keep cool.

Slide the chapa or plancha away from the fire and in its place lay the apple wedges. Grill them for 2–3 minutes on each side, until golden and lightly caramelized. Transfer to a small fireproof tin, slide the chapa back over the direct heat, then rest the apples on the grill bars away from the fire to keep warm.

Melt the knob of butter on the hot chapa, using scrunched-up paper towel to spread it out in a thin layer. Use a metal spatula to lift the brioche onto the chapa and shut the barbecue lid. Leave to cook for 2 minutes, or until set and lightly golden, then flip over to cook the other side.

Serve the French toast with the apples on the side and the whipped cream spooned on top.

Serves 4
–
Direct +
Indirect
Cooking

GRILLED PINEAPPLE WITH CHILLI & RUM BUTTER SAUCE v

A totally tropical take on a pineapple. The rum is optional, so replace it with orange juice for an alcohol-free version.

1 medium pineapple
100g (7 tbsp) butter
3 tbsp soft brown sugar
3 tbsp rum (or orange juice)
1–2 hot red chillies, to taste
vanilla ice cream, to serve

Fire up the barbecue ready for direct grilling (see page 9). Once hot, give the grill bars a good scrub with a wire brush.

Use a large sharp knife to chop off the top and bottom of the pineapple, then slice down in thin strips to remove the peel. The pineapple will now be left with lots of unsightly brown eyes that you don't want to eat. You will see that the eyes are in spiral lines running diagonally around the pineapple.

Turn the pineapple on its side, take a small sharp knife and cut a deep V-shaped trench down either side of each row of eyes, removing the row in one piece. Rotate the pineapple and move onto the next row. Repeat until all the eyes are removed. Cut the pineapple into 1cm (½in) thick slices.

Put the butter, sugar, rum (or orange juice) and chillies in a small fireproof tin or pan (no plastic or wooden handles) and rest on the grill bars, slightly away from the fire, and leave to melt.

Lay the pineapple slices on the grill bars directly above the fire. Use a silicone pastry brush (see page 7) to baste the pineapple with the butter and rum sauce as it grills, turning regularly until the slices are deeply caramelized. Once the pineapple is cooked, lift each slice into the tin and toss in the remaining sauce.

Serve a couple of slices of hot pineapple on each plate, top with a scoop of ice cream, drizzle over the remaining sauce and tuck in.

Serves 4
–
Direct Cooking

MARSHMALLOW, CHOCOLATE & STRAWBERRY 'MESS' v

A gooey and stickily irresistible sharing pudding, more of an idea to experiment with than a recipe to follow.

150g (5½oz) marshmallows (vegetarian, if need be)
200g (7oz) strawberries, halved
8 chocolate-covered biscuits (cookies) (I use Choco Leibniz)
8 plain digestive biscuits (4½oz Graham Crackers)
a handful of hazelnuts, roughly chopped

This is designed to be cooked once you have finished cooking everything else on your barbecue, cooking on gently glowing embers rather than a full-on fire.

Scatter the marshmallows over the base of a fireproof pan (no wooden or plastic handles). A small roasting tin or frying pan (skillet) is ideal. Tuck in the strawberry halves. Snap both types of biscuit in half and tuck them in. Finish with a sprinkle of chopped hazelnuts.

Set the tin onto the barbecue slightly away from the remaining fire so that the marshmallows and chocolate on the biscuits (cookies) begin to melt. You can cook this for as long or short as you like. Eat it when the marshmallows are still firm or cook it for longer, during which time the base will caramelize and crisp up. Do keep an eye on it though as it will burn easily if it gets too hot.

Allow to cool a little before tucking in with spoons, forks or fingers.

Other ways to serve your 'mess':

Use sliced peaches instead of strawberries.

Tuck in a few squares of chocolate or caramel.

Swap the hazelnuts for pecans or macadamia nuts.

Experiment with different types of biscuits.

Serves 4–6
–
Indirect Cooking

BROWNIE WITH PECANS & WHITE CHOCOLATE v

The trick to this fudgy brownie is an indirect heat and a cooling barbecue, and you will definitely need a barbecue with a lid. With good charcoal and a clean grill there should be no smoky taste as charcoal doesn't smoke.

250g (1 cup) butter, softened
350g (1¾ cup) caster
(superfine) sugar
4 large eggs
100g (¾ cup) self raising
(self rising) flour
75g (¾ cup) cocoa (unsweetened
chocolate) powder
2 tsp vanilla extract
90g (3¼oz) white chocolate,
roughly chopped
50g (½ cup) pecans,
roughly chopped

Line a fireproof tin measuring 20 × 25cm (8 × 10in) with baking parchment, pressing it right into the corners.

The brownie will cook best when your barbecue is at 200–225°C (390–440°F). If your barbecue doesn't have a temperature gauge on the lid, test using an oven thermometer. You don't want a raging fire, but a pile of glowing embers to one side of the grill and no fire on the other, so you can cook indirectly.

In a large mixing bowl, mix the softened butter, caster (superfine) sugar, eggs, flour, cocoa (unsweetened chocolate) powder and vanilla. Use an electric whisk to beat everything together until thick and smooth. If the butter is very soft, almost melting, you can do this easily using a wooden spoon and a little elbow grease.

Scoop the brownie mixture into the lined tin, using the flat blade of a table knife to level it. At this point you can cover the tin and put it in the fridge for 1–2 hours until you are ready to cook, or you can take straight to the barbecue.

When you are ready to cook, slide the tin onto the grill bars away from the direct fire and shut the lid. Cook for 30 minutes, turning the tin a couple of times to make sure it is baking evenly.

Lift the lid and quickly scatter the chopped chocolate and pecans over the surface then shut the lid again and cook for a further 30 minutes or so. It is ready when the surface feels set and it is firm to touch around the edges but with plenty of squish in the centre.

Leave the brownie to cool and firm up for 30 minutes.

Makes
12–16
–
Indirect
Cooking

INDEX

ACKNOWLEDGEMENTS

Books are the ultimate collaboration, with many people working together as a team to create what you now hold in your hands. At Quadrille, I would love to thank Sarah Lavelle for entrusting me with another book, to Stacey Cleworth for her eagle editor's eye, Emily Lapworth for her beautiful design, Susan Low for her thorough copy-editing and Kate Jarvis for making sure everything prints out just so.

I know how pictures enhance and add to the enjoyment and usefulness of a cookbook, bringing the recipes alive to inspire you to cook the dishes. So a massive thanks to Jason Ingram whose gorgeous work you see here. It's always such a pleasure to work with you, come rain or shine! Thanks to Imke Potgieter for her fabulous assisting skills on shoot days – I know a grafter when I meet one, and you cook like a demon! Thanks to Jaine for her boxes and boxes of lovely props.

Thanks to Martine Carter, my agent, for her unwavering support and encouragement.

Being part of the BBQ and fire cooking community is a truly wonderful thing; never have I met such a supportive and encouraging bunch. Huge thanks and many, many hugs go out to my Fire Tribe, you know who you are, I love you all. Let the good times roll.

Even bigger love goes to my Home Tribe – Rob, Izaac and Eve – thank you for letting me be me and for your enduring support even when my head is swimming on an entirely different plane ;-).

Finally, a big thank you to YOU, for cooking from *Foolproof BBQ*. Nothing makes this author happier than knowing her books are well thumbed and covered in splats from good use. Do share your cooks with me over on social media, I just love seeing what you make.

Happy grilling!
@GenevieveEats